Gestalt Therapy on

The Gestalt Therapy Page is the comprehensive web resource for information, resources, publications relating to the theory and practice of Gestalt therapy.

Visitors can subscribe to News and Notes, a free email calendar of conferences, training programs, and other events of interest to the worldwide Gestalt therapy community.

The Gestalt Therapy Page includes an on-line store that offers the most comprehensive collection of books and recordings available – many available nowhere else!

Visit today: www.gestalt.org

The Gestalt Journal Press was founded in 1975 and is currently the leading publisher and distributor of books, journals, and educational recordings relating to the theory and practice of Gestalt therapy. Our list of titles includes new editions of all the classic works by Frederick Perls, Laura Perls, Paul Goodman, Ralph Hefferline, and Jan Christiaan Smuts. Our catalog also includes a wide variety of books by contemporary theoreticians and clinicians including Richard Hycner, Lynne Jacobs, Violet Oaklander, Peter Phillipson, Erving & Miriam Polster, Edward W. L. Smith, and Gary Yontef.

In 1976, we began publication of The Gestalt Journal (now the International Gestalt Journal), the first professional periodical devoted exclusively to the theory and practice of Gestalt therapy.

Our collection of video and audio recordings features the works of Frederick (Fritz) and Laura Perls, Violet Oaklander, Erving & Miriam Polster, Janie Rhyne, and James Simkin.

The Gestalt Journal Press, in conjunction with the University of California, Santa Barbara, maintains the world's largest archive of Gestalt therapy related materials including original manuscripts and correspondence, published and unpublished, by Gestalt therapy pioneers Frederick & Laura Perls and Paul Goodman. The archives also include more than six thousand hours of audio and video recordings of presentations, panels and interviews dating to early 1961.

Gestalt Therapy

MINI-LECTURES

James S. Simkin, Ph.D.

Edited by
Abraham Levitsky, Ph.D.
and Zoe Snyder, M.S.W.

With a new introduction by Erving Polster, Ph.D

———————— § ————————

A Publication of THE GESTALT LEGACY PRESS

A Publication of The Gestalt Legacy Press

Copyright © 1976, 1974 by James S. Simkin, Ph.D.
Copyright © 2005 by The Gestalt Legacy Press

Published by:

The Gestalt Legacy Press, Inc.
A Division of:
The Center for Gestalt Development, Inc.
P. O. Box 278
Gouldsboro ME 04607-0278
U.S.A.

ISBN 978-1-892966-01-8

Contents

Introduction to The Gestalt Journal Edition

Gestalt Therapy Mini-Lectures is a sprinkling of James Simkin's observations on a number of important psychological concerns, many of which reflect the doctrinal battlegrounds of the 1960's and serve as a memorandum of the ideological critique represented in early Gestalt work. In those days people had strengthened their drive to cut through the cultural imperatives of their times. The frustration of fixed marriages, burdensome careerism, hypocritical morality, and tired coping; all were opposed by methodological transformations which encouraged an incredible optimism that people could take their lives into their own hands, setting their constrictions aside, and change anything.

A most powerful instrument of this optimism, one which helped shape the history of psychotherapy, was Frederick Perls' advocacy of therapeutic pointedness by heightening the concentration on one's own experience and heightening the contact with other people. The accompanying emphasis on focal experience was a hypnotic-like innovation and served as a breakthrough into therapeutic simplicity. Though this emphasis was not faithful to the broader principles of Gestalt therapy, which stressed the importance of context and contradiction, it nevertheless served as a bright spotlight on any experience when the experience was freed from the often paralyzing complexities of existence. The excision of much of the ordinary spread of personal concerns, the there-and-then, opened many eyes to the satori-like psychological power of highly focussed simplicity. This specialized attention was more than an evasion of a larger reality; it was a resounding entry into restricted regions of the mind. Clarity of perception, empowerment in action, and openness to previously disabling fears were among the benefits generated by pointedness and the narrowing of life context.

Jim Simkin was a master of incisiveness and simplicity and he found a sharp instrument in the Perlsian emphasis. At first, the conceptual association between the two of them was extremely close but over the years Simkin tempered his identification with Perls, who had come to disregard many of the basic precepts of his own theory. In this book, the reader may glimpse Simkin's struggles to free himself of some of the more strangling misconceptions of the 60's version of Gestalt therapy. As one example, he parts company with the Perlsian view that people, ideally, would be only self supportive and he recognizes the centrality of environmental support in everyone's life. This crucial recognition had implications for a softening of the therapeutic engagement; adding a conversational component, ordinary curiosity, kindness and less commanding tension development.

However, at other points in this book, Simkin slips into the simplified shibboleths of the day. He says, for example, "The way to be is to be you... You have a right to be in this world the way you are; there is *plenty of room in this world for everybody.*" However valuable this maxim may be to many people, the advantages of being one's self will offer small consolation to people in unchanging misery. Whether there is room or not to be what you are often depends on the will of existing authority, the niggardliness of geographical happenstance or the fixity of internal contradiction. The need to change is always there, in tension with the need to be as one already is. To encourage one over the other is only half the story, a concession to the temptations of simplicity.

The exclusion of "shoulds" is another example of a simplified principle with which Simkin struggles. Although it is therapeutically mobilizing for many people to eliminate the shoulds in their lives, this maxim often neglects certain natural dilemmas. Aren't "shoulds" indispensable in trying to integrate competing wishes? Clearly, if I *want* to succeed in my work, I *should* get up on time in the morning, whether I *want* to or not. Simkin was a man of considerable discipline and clearly knew the value of prioritizing one's wishes. But he wanted so much to emphasize the transformation of shoulds into wants that his disdain for shoulds served unintentionally to discredit preestablished purpose and discipline.

One might well ask if simplification is inevitable in the early stages of any method; if one can communicate to large numbers of people while maintaining a yes-but-on-the-other-hand attitude about telling the whole story. Would the recital of complexities water down a theory, making it so thin that it no longer commands attention? Do simple concepts register most clearly with people and get them on the road to facing neglected concerns? Simple concepts, do, indeed, light the way toward the management of complexities which must, after all, be reduced to identifiable and assimilable elements.

However, the special advantages of simplification must be understood. The surgeon who drapes all of the patient's body areas except the point of incision does so to prevent distraction. Yet, he must also know there is more to the body than his point of incision. The orthodox psychoanalyst who insists on being only ambiguously present is making a special arrangement for improving the identifiability of transference. Yet, he must know that in spite of his technique, there is a "real" engagement going on with his patient anyway. The Gestalt therapist who sees hidden negativism in the word, "but," tells his patient that instead of saying "I would like to come to dinner *but* I have another commitment," just leave out what comes before the "but." That may often be therapeutically valuable to someone whose negations are thus amplified into recognizability. *But*, what one leaves out is the complexity of choice, the common decency of an explanatory, friendly response, and the acknowledgement of contrast. The need adequately to express complexity, decency, and contrast — essential in the human mind — can be obscured only temporarily.

In my many contacts with Simkin over the years (we taught frequently in each other's training programs) it was evident this struggle between the simple and the complex engaged him until his death in 1984. That struggle and many other changes in him over the intervening years are only partially reflected in this book, published in 1973. The book does, nevertheless, provide a view into the mind of one of the magnificent therapists of his day, one whose work gave honor to the concepts he describes. Jim Simkin was a therapeutic stylist who demonstrated the powerful leverage of high attention, accurate perceptions, honesty, common sense, and a talent for saying the timely word. He became a wizard among the many people he taught, continually offering cunning confrontations to the mysteries he witnessed. These mysteries enthralled him to the end; yet one of his prime accomplishments was to demystify the mysterious by turning it into common human experience, understandable and assimilable. The reader will see this process manifested over and over in this book.

Erving Polster
San Diego, California
January, 1990

Author's Preface

Shortly after I began to lead workshops in Gestalt therapy along with the late Fritz Perls in 1964, I developed a style of mini-lecturing — originally called coattailing — following some work with a patient or Gestalt therapy trainee.

Since 1967 some of the mini-lectures have been audio taped and from time to time collated on one or more tapes and/or transcribed. In 1970 Joy Robinson took a number of these tapes and prepared typed copies with the eventual aim of editing a book of mini-lectures. The following year she returned the project to me and during 1972 - 1973 my friend and colleague Abe Levitsky has been editing and collating the mini-lectures.

I have added two chapters; the first introduces Gestalt therapy to the uninitiated and the second presents an example of some of my clinical work.

My wife, Anne, is responsible for originally collecting my mini-lectures and urging the preparation of this book, To her, I gratefully dedicate my first complete book in Gestalt therapy.

James S. Simkin, Ph.D.
Big Sur, California

Introduction to the Revised Edition

A proliferation of books and articles in Gestalt therapy marks the decade of the 1070's. In addition to both popular and technical works, an impressive Gestalt therapy literature is beginning to appear in academic journals and in the number and quality of (both Master's and Doctoral) dissertations.

I have appended a partial bibliography of this burgeoning literature to give the reader a sampling of what has been typical of the first half of the '70's and in all probability will continue to occur during the later half.

An additional phenomenon has been the establishment of Gestalt therapy as the third most popular form of psychotherapy as practiced in the '70's. (Psychoanalysis or psychoanalytically oriented psychotherapy is still no. 1, followed by behavior modification.)

In the late 1960's I wrote my "Introduction to Gestalt Therapy" paper. Originally this was to appear in a book by Jurjevich around 1969 - 1970. The paper did finally appear in his two volume *Direct Psychotherapy: 28 American Originals,* as chapter fifteen of volume 1, published in 1973. A modification of that paper was given to Stephenson in 1972 and appeared in his *Gestalt Therapy Primer* in 1975 as chapter I. The same paper, somewhat edited, also appeared as chapter 3 in Brown's, *The Live Classroom.* I believe he had requested it in 1973. A further revision and extension of the paper was prepared in 1970 for Gazda's *Basic Approaches to Group Psychotherapy and Group Counseling,* 2nd Edition. It was published in 1975 and the chapter is entitled "Gestalt Therapy in

Groups" — chapter XI. A somewhat abbreviated version of this paper appears in this book as well as in the book's original edition. And a variation of this paper called "Gestalt Psychotherapy," also appeared in Bannister's *Issues and Approaches in the Psychological Therapies*, 1975.

The demand for *a* chapter on Gestalt therapy shows a dramatic increase in the early to mid '70's. In the same period, I have also turned down requests for a chapter on Gestalt therapy on the average of twice a year.

In this revised edition I have added a longer sample of my clinical work, section V, as well as adding a more recent mini-lecture.

James S. Simkin, Ph.D.
Big Sur, California

Gestalt Therapy Mini-lectures

Gestalt Therapy in Groups

Gestalt Therapy in Groups

Gestalt is a German word meaning whole or configuration. As one psychological dictionary puts it, ". . . an *integration* of members as contrasted with a summation of parts" (Warren, 1934, p. 115). The term also implies a unique kind of psychotherapy as formulated by the late Frederick S. Perls, his co-workers, and his followers.

Dr. Perls began, as did many of his colleagues in those days, as a psychoanalyst, after having been trained as a physician in Post-World War I Germany. In 1926 he worked under Professor Kurt Goldstein at the Frankfurt Neurological Institute where he was first exposed to the tenets of Gestalt psychology but ". . . was still too preoccupied with the orthodox approach to assimilate more than a fraction of what was offered" (Perls, 1947, p. 5). Later, Dr. Perls was exposed to the theories and practice of Wilhelm Reich and incorporated some of the concepts and techniques of character analysis into his work.

While serving as a Captain in the South African Medical Corps, Perls wrote his first manuscript in 1941–1942 outlining his emerging theory and application of personality in-

15

tegration which later appeared as a book, *Ego, Hunger and Aggression*. The term "Gestalt Therapy" was first used in 1949 as the title of a book on Perls' methods written by him and two co-authors, Ralph Hefferline of Columbia University and the late Paul Goodman of New York City.

Group Psychotherapy and Workshops

In Gestalt therapy the emphasis is on the present, ongoing situation, which, of course, involves the interaction of at least two people—in individual therapy, the patient and the therapist. This interaction becomes expanded to more than two people in the group situation and may involve the inter-active process among several people or may involve the interactive process at any given moment between two people with each of the other participants involving themselves as they are ready. In Gestalt therapy it is not necessary to emphasize the group dynamics, although some Gestalt therapists do so. All Gestalt therapists focus at one time or another on the interactive process between the therapist and the group member in the here and now and/or the interactive process between group members as it is ongoing.

Perls preferred the term *workshop* to *group psychotherapy* and in a paper written in 1967 indicated the values of workshop versus individual therapy as follows:

> To the whole group it is obvious that the person in distress does not see the obvious, does not see the way out of the impasse, does not see (for instance) that his whole misery is a purely imagined one. In the face of this collective conviction he cannot use his usual phobic way of disowning the therapist when he cannot manipulate him . . . . Behind the impasse . . . is the catastrophic expectation. . . . In the safe emergency of the therapeutic situation, he (the patient) discovers that the world does not fall to pieces if he gets angry, sexy, joyous, or mournful. The group supports his self-esteem. The appreciation of his

achievements toward authenticity and greater liveliness also is not to be underestimated. Gestalt therapists also use the group for doing collective experiments in learning to understand the importance of the atmosphere. . . . The observation by the group members of the manipulative games of playing helpless, stupid, wailing, seductive or other roles by which the neurotic helps himself in the infantile state of controlling, facilitates their own recognition. (1967, p. 17).

Theoretical Foundations

Man is considered a total organism functioning as a whole, rather than an entity split into dichotomies such as mind and body. With the philosophical background of humanism, *a la* Otto Rank, the organism is seen as born with the capacity to cope with life. This is opposed to what I call the "original sin theory of human development"—that the organism must learn to repress or supress its instinctual strivings in order to become "civilized." The emergence of existential philosophy coincides historically with the development of Gestalt therapy. Wilson Van Dusen (1960), in an article on existential analytic psychotherapy, believes that there is only one psychotherapeutic approach which unites the phenomenological approach with existential theory, and that is Gestalt therapy.

The theoretical model of the psychodynamic schools of personality—chiefly the Freudian school—envisions the personality like an onion consisting of layers. Each time a layer is peeled away, there is still another layer until you finally come to the core. (Incidentally, in the process of "analysis" of the onion, you may have very little or nothing left by the time you come to the core!) I envision the personality more like a rubber ball which has only a thick outer layer and is empty inside. The ball floats or swims in an environment so that at any given moment only a portion is exposed while the rest is submerged in the water. Thus, rather than inventing an unconscious or preconscious to account for behavior that we are unaware of, I suggest that unaware behavior is the result of the organism not being in touch with its external environment due to its being mostly submerged in its own background (internal environment), or fantasies.

In *A Review of the Practice of Gestalt Therapy,* Yontef (1971) summarized the theory of Gestalt therapy. He reasoned that organismic needs lead to sensory motor behavior. Once a configuration is formed which has the qualities of a good gestalt, the organismic need which has been foreground is met and a balance or state of satiation or no-need is achieved.

> When a need is met, the Gestalt it organized becomes complete and it no longer exerts an influence—the organism is free to form new gestalten. When this gestalt formation and destruction are blocked or rigidified at any stage, when needs are not recognized and expressed, the flexible harmony and flow of the organism/environment field is disturbed. Unmet needs form incomplete gestalten that clamor for attention and, therefore, interfere with the formation of new gestalten (Yontef, p. 3).

As Perls (1948) puts it, "The most important fact about the figure-background formation is that if a need is genuinely satisfied, the situation is changed" (p. 571).

Example of a First Session
in a Gestalt Workshop

The following excerpt is an example of how one workshop started. Following a short introduction, a suggested exercise involved each of the participants and very quickly one of the participants asked to work.

Jim: Good evening. I'd like to start with a few sentences about contract and then suggest an exercise. I believe that there are no "shoulds" in

Gestalt therapy. What you do is what you do. What I do is what I do. I do have a preference. I prefer that you be straight with me. *Please* remember, this is a preference, not a should. If you feel that you *should* honor my preference then that's *your* should! When I ask you, "Where are you?" my preference is that you tell me—or tell me that you're not willing to tell me. Then our transaction is straight. Any time that you want to know where I am, please ask me. I will either tell you, or tell you I am unwilling to tell you—so that our transaction will be straight.

Now for the exercise. Please look around the room and select someone you don't know or don't know well—whom you would like to know better . . . O.K.? Now here are the rules. You may do anything you like to "know" the other person better, except talk! John?

John:	The lady with the brown sweater.
Jim:	Marilyn, are you willing to be "known" by John?
Marilyn:	Yes.
Jim:	Elaine, please select a partner.
Elaine:	That man—I believe he said his name was Bert.
Jim:	Are you willing, Bert?
Bert:	My pleasure!
Jim:	Nancy?
Nancy:	I would like to know Agnes better.
Agnes:	That's fine with me.
Jon:	Well, that leaves me to Phil.
Jim:	Yes, unless you're willing to include me.
Jon:	No thanks. I'd rather get to know Phil! [Group laughter.]

The group breaks into dyads and for several minutes the person who has asked to know the other is the aggressor "exploring" the other with his sensory modalities (touch, taste, smell, etc.), lifting, pulling, dancing with, etc. Then the partners in the dyad are asked to switch and the "aggressor" becomes the "aggressee" as the exercise is repeated.

Jim: O.K., I am interested in knowing more about your experience. If you have made any discoveries about *yourself* and are willing to share, please tell the rest of us what you found out.

Bert: I discovered that I felt very awkward and uncomfortable when Elaine was the aggressor!

Elaine: I sensed your discomfort and found myself concerned with what you thought of me.

Bert: I would like to work on my always having to be "masculine"—my avoidance of my passivity.

Jim: When?

Bert: Now! [At this point Bert leaves his chair in the circle and sits in the empty chair across from the therapist.]

I feel anxious. My heart is pounding and my hands feel sweaty, and I'm aware of all of the others in the room.

Jim: Is there anything you would like to say to the others?

For the next 15-20 minutes Bert worked in the "hot-seat." When he finished the therapist turned his focus (awareness) back to the group.

In the Now

The following example is taken from my training film, *In the Now.* After my introductory comments, Al moved from the group circle to the "hot-seat." He was very eager to start. His work with me is presented verbatim from the film.

Jim: Okay, now I would suggest we start getting in touch with what we're doing in this situation now. Most people are interested, or at least they say they are interested, in changing their behavior. This is what therapy is all about. In order to change behavior, you have to know what you're doing and how you do what you do. So, let's start with your examining, focusing your awareness and saying what you're experiencing.

Al: I feel as though I got the catastrophe by sitting over there suffering, and I still feel it at intervals. But I really haven't felt so much like a patient in all the time I've been a psychologist. I think it's for this special occasion. Last night at four o'clock in the morning I awoke . . . well, it started at nine . . . I started blushing in the groin, you know. I thought it was a flea bite 'cause we got five new dogs . . . pups. I couldn't find the flea. By four o'clock in the morning, I was blushing here and here, in my head, and I couldn't sleep. I was itching so. And I got an antihistamine. By nine or ten in the morning the itching went away and then coming here I get this chest . . . my chest hurts.

Jim: How about right now?

Al: I'm sweating. I sweat and I'm warm.

Jim: What happened to your voice?

Al: It got low and warm and I wiggle a little.

Jim: And now?

Al: I feel a tension I carry around a good deal up here—a band that grabs my head like that and pulls me together like I'm puzzled.

Jim: Play the band that's pulling on Al. "I am Al's band and I . . ."

Al:	I am Al's band containing him. I'm his crazy megalomania—want to run the world his way.
Jim:	Tell Al what your objections are to his running the world his way.
Al:	He's a nut . . . to think he can run the world his way. Or a child.
Jim:	Now give Al a voice and let Al talk to the band.
Al:	I know how to run it as well as anybody else. Why shouldn't I.
Jim:	You sounded like a fairly reasonable nut or child at that moment . . . and now?
Al:	Back to my gut. I make myself suffer to recognize I can't take what I want.
Jim:	Okay, what is it that you want that you're not taking at this moment?
Al:	Well, I very reluctantly thought of the milk and the world as one.
Jim:	You're reluctantly not taking the milk and the world at this moment.
Al:	I'm sure that's not what I said. I reluctantly *thought* of the milk. I didn't want to talk about that. I'd rather be a megalomaniac than an infant asking for warmth (mother's milk).
Jim:	Can you imagine anything in between those two . . . the infant and the megalomaniac?
Al:	It's a long way, yeah. You know I'm an extremist. Let's see a bite size. Yeah, how about just writing an article on art therapy, which I've scheduled for the last three years? I haven't done that. I would like it just to flow and to come out without any pain, without giving up anything else.
Jim:	So you want to be the breast.

Al: I want to be the breast? To be a giver, to flow. Oh well, I hadn't thought of it that way.

Jim: Well, think of it that way. Take a couple of hours. Imagine yourself a big tit.

Al: It's a very feminine thing to be, a breast.

Jim: Yeah.

Al: Give a little . . . . Give a lot.

Jim: Yeah.

Al: You get . . . you capture your son with that milk. You hold onto him.

Jim: Al?

Al: Yeah?

Jim: Would you be willing to be as tender, soft, feminine as you know how?

Al: It's a threat.

Jim: What's a threat?

Al: To follow your suggestion would be a threat . . . of what? Makes no sense.

Jim: Okay. Do the opposite. Whatever the reverse of being soft, tender, loving, feminine is for you.

Al: Be masculine.

Jim: Show me.

Al: It's something like *"practice"* . . . you know fatherly, uh *"shut-up!*

Jim: Yeah, do a little scowling with it. That's it.

Al: *"Shut up!"* So it's not puzzling, it's uh, it's father. *"You burnt the soup!"* *"Leave the table,"* and then a kind of fantasy of mother crying. I sort of regret that my father died before I became friendly with him again.

Jim: Say this to him.

Al:	I'm sorry. [sigh] Well, inside I said I'm sorry you died.
Jim:	Outside.
Al:	I'm sorry.
Jim:	Say this to him outside.
Al:	I'm sorry you died too soon [for me].
Jim:	Give him a voice.
Al:	I haven't the slightest idea what he would say. I thought of his excusing me. He says, "You, you didn't know any better. You were young and angry."
Jim:	Your father sounds tender.
Al:	He may be the father I wanted. I never, I don't think of him as a tender man but . . .
Jim:	It's the voice you gave him.
Al:	Yeah. I may have underestimated him.
Jim:	Say this to him.
Al:	Dad, I guess I did, I underestimated you.
Jim:	Say this to Al.
Al:	Al, you underestimated me. You could have been closer . . .
Jim:	[Interrupts] No, no. Say this sentence to Al. "Al, I underestimate you."
Al:	Al, I underestimate you. You can do a good deal more than you're doing. Then I put myself down and say, "You're crazy to expect so much from yourself," and don't do anything . . . like going from do everything to do nothing. Just sit and don't create it. I feel a little phony to accept your interpretation so easily.
Jim:	You see what you just did?
Al:	I puzzled myself?

Jim:	You said, "I feel a little phony . . ." There came your band.
Al:	And it hurts here (points to chest). It didn't hurt there for a long time. What happened? I'm supposed to know? So I've got a blind spot. I'm entitled.
Jim:	Your blind spot happens to be Al Freeman.
Al:	A total blind spot?
Jim:	You're not entitled to that blind spot. What are you doing?
Al:	Puzzling. You're playing God and telling me I'm not. I'm not God? That was a . . . I didn't expect to say that at all, really.
Jim:	What just happened?
Al:	I exposed something, I guess. It was quite unintended.
Jim:	Yeah.
Al:	I was just going to argue with you, and I came out with my manic side. I don't often do that.
Jim:	You just did.
Al:	It slipped. I'm sorry . . . I'm not sorry, I'm glad, I'm glad. Whew.
Jim:	What do you experience right now?
Al:	Warmth. I love having people laugh, especially with me. So I guess everybody wants it. Wants warmth and the approval and the closeness.
Jim:	O.K. Play God a little while longer and give Al warmth and closeness.
Al:	I would never have thought of that . . . O.K. . . . God talking: "Al, you've been deprived, so you must have warmth and love."
Jim:	Uh-uh! God never makes excuses or gives reasons.

Al: No?

Jim: I know.

Al: I give you permission to be God. I understand. Yeah, you have warmth. I give you . . . I give you warmth. What else do you want? The world? You can have the world. Just be sure to give it back . . . in ten minutes. God is an impostor, because I'm God. And that other one is a fake. I really could do the whole thing myself.

Jim: Yeah. Now you're catching on.

Therapist-Patient Relationship

Although some people claim they want to change their behavior, I believe that most people seeking psychotherapy want relief from discomfort. This may be generalized malaise—anxiety, depression, and the like—or very specific discomfort like headache, stiff neck, knotted stomach, etc. Furthermore, their usual expectation is that relief will be the result of the therapist doing the work, rather than through their own efforts.

Ideally, I see myself as a midwife in relationship to my patient. Having been present at many "births" of new attitudes, feelings, conceptualizations, behavior and the like (including my own), I can facilitate acceptance (re-owning) of these attitudes, feelings, etc. on the part of the patient through my acceptance of where the patient and I are at the moment. My "of course" attitude can be reassuring to the person I'm relating to as well as facilitate change through non-pushing.

At times, my relationship to my patient is that of a senior experimenter or scientist to the junior or novice experimenter. At other times, we are both risking (experimenting) taking steps into the unknown and momentarily relinquishing centeredness in the quest for growth and the excitement of growth.

I see each therapeutic encounter with my patient as a separate gestalt. An event which can be complex unto itself and has the potential of a structure with a beginning, a middle and an end. Whatever is foreground at the beginning of a session is what is focused on and worked with—be it a rehearsed program, an immediate awareness of some sensory or motor experience, a feeling of confusion, recall of unfinished business, etc.

Research in the Area of Gestalt Therapy

There has been relatively little research in Gestalt therapy. Commenting on the difficulties in doing research in this area, Fagan and Shepherd say:

> Most often, hard data are difficult to obtain: the important variables resist quantification; the complexity and multiplicity of variables in therapist, patient, and the interactional processes are almost impossible to unravel; and the crudeness and restrictiveness of the measuring devices available cannot adequately reflect the subtlety of the process. However, the fact that the task is difficult does not reduce its importance, and the need for many questions to be asked and answered by the more formal procedures available to researchers (Fagan and Shepherd, 1970, p. 241.)

I have been interested in assessing the effectiveness of Gestalt therapy in workshops as contrasted with weekly therapy. During the years 1970 and 1971, I developed some clinical impressions in the form of feedback from people coming to residential workshops, and I compared the feedback of these patients with feedback that I obtained from patients whom I had been seeing in a more traditional manner the previous two years. Seventy-five percent of the patients who attended the residential workshop reported that they received what they came for or more. This claim was made by 66 percent of those who were in weekly therapy with me.

The percentage of patients who claimed that they received no help, or got worse, was approximately equal for those coming to residential workshops and those coming for weekly therapy (14 percent). The remainder in both the traditional and the workshop style were people who claimed they "got something" from the experience. (It is interesting to note that patients who had either the invidual or group work on a "spaced" basis and the workshop on a "massed" basis favor the massed basis by a ratio of about 9 to 1.) Feedback data have been obtained from over 200 people who have attended both workshops and traditional therapy.

I have also experimented with training in Gestalt therapy and have data on the results of an experiment massing close to 300 hours of training into a three-month period. What I attempted was to provide an intensive training experience for five therapists in a residential setting. The number of hours available was comparable to (or more than) the number of hours of training in the more formal training institutes. Using personality inventories, peer group ratings, the A.B. Therapists Scale, my clinical impressions of the trainees and other measurements, I have some preliminary evidence which supports the possibility of successfully massing training in a three-month period. A follow-up study, in which the five therapists returned for a week, seven months after their training, indicated that the *direction* of change (shown during the three-month period) continued. In addition the quality of their work in dealing with patients showed a consistent positive increase as reflected by both patient's and supervisor's rating of their work.

Yontef (1969) discusses some of the possible research areas in Gestalt therapy. He also discusses the attitudes of Perls and his co-workers concerning research (pp. 39–40).

Goals

In Gestalt therapy the patient is taught to use awareness in the service of himself as a total functioning organism. By learning to focus awareness and thus discovering what *is,* rather than what *should be,* or what *could have been,* or the ideal of what *may be,* the patient learns to trust himself. This is called in Gestalt therapy the optimum development of self-support. Through awareness, the splits which have been developed can be reintegrated. The patient can become more whole as he begins to deal with his avoidances, which have created holes in her personality.

I sometimes will use the simile of a cake in encouraging patients to re-own the parts of themselves which they have considered noxious or otherwise unacceptable. Just as the oil, or flour or baking powder, etc., by themselves can be distasteful, as part of the whole cake they are indispensable to assure its success.

Selection and Group Composition

During the period from 1960 through 1970, I led a wide variety of ongoing groups. These were general psycho-therapy groups, psychotherapy groups for couples, and training groups in Gestalt therapy. All of the patients in the therapy groups were previously patients in individual Gestalt therapy. The range of time that a person was in individual treatment prior to entering a group was anywhere from a few sessions to two or three years. Each therapy group was balanced with an equal number of male and female patients. Attempts were made to insure the heterogeneity of the groups by bringing in as wide a range of age, occupation, presenting problems, etc., as was possible from the sources available. One typical group had an actor, a student, two housewives, a physicist, an x-ray technician, an attorney, a nurse, a drama coach, a psychologist, and a painter. The age range for this group was from the early twenties to the late fifties. There were equal numbers of men and women.

Frequency, Length, and Duration of Groups

Groups would meet once a week for a two-hour session. Occasionally the larger groups would continue beyond two hours. All of the above-mentioned groups were open-ended with the exception of the couples group which was a closed group.

Approximately one-third of the group patients were also seen in individual therapy on a once a week basis or less frequently. None of the couples were in individual therapy concurrently and only one of the therapists was in regular individual treatment.

The typical group patient had about 70 to 80 hours of group treatment over a period of eight months to a year. Some group members were able to terminate treatment within three to six months (25–50 hours of therapy); others had been in group as long as three years when I discontinued practice in Beverly Hills.

The training groups began with one group in 1968. By 1969 there were two and these continued until I left southern California in July of 1970. Average attendance in these groups was 30 sessions (60 hours). However, many of the therapists in training also participated in five-day workshops with me at the Esalen Institute.

The couples group began in the fall of 1969 and terminated at the end of June 1970. Average attendance for this group was 25 sessions (50 to 60 therapy hours). One couple terminated before the group stopped.

Selection and Composition of Groups

The therapist reserved the right to bring new people into the training groups and the therapy groups. The participants in the therapy groups, however, could veto, during the initial session, the continued participation of a new member. This veto was not available to the therapists in training. In the couples group there had to be a unanimous agreement on the part of all couples, including the therapist and his wife, for the introduction of a new couple into the closed group.

In the training groups, all of the therapists in training were licensed or license-eligible psychiatrists, clinical psychologists or social workers with the exception of two school psychologists whose function included group counseling in the school system. In the training groups there was also an attempt to keep a balance of the sexes. However, this was not always possible because there are more males than females in the helping professions. There was also a preponderence of psychologists in the training group. Audiotape was used in all three groups and occasionally videotape was available for some of the work.

Psychotherapists who wanted to participate in the training groups were required to have a minimum of one individual session to determine their suitability for training and working within the Gestalt therapy framework. Sometimes I would recommend personal therapy rather than training. At other times I would suggest concurrent therapy with the training. Some of the psychotherapists were admitted for training without being required to seek personal therapy.

Gestalt Therapist Qualifications

The typical Gestalt therapist who is currently being trained at one of the existing Gestalt therapy institutes is a licensed or license-eligible psychotherapist usually from one of the three major disciplines which are licensed to practice psychotherapy in the United States. In most states these are psychiatrists, clinical psychologists and clinical social workers. Typically, the Gestalt therapist is trained in an institute or in a closely supervised apprenticeship with a senior Gestalt therapist over a period of several months to two or three years.

I am currently experimenting with several one-month intensive training programs to see whether it is possible to train Gestalt therapists via this modality as opposed to the more traditional spaced learning situations offered at the Gestalt therapy institutes throughout the country. In the spaced learning model, the Gestalt therapist trainee typically works two to four hours a week in both group and individual settings. In addition to a didactic or theoretical seminar once a month, he is required to attend a minimum of a weekend or a longer workshop every two or three months. At some of the Gestalt therapy institutes, the advanced trainees co-lead introductory seminars with institute members, as part of their experiential training.

Workshop Style—Training/Treatment

A good deal of the work done in Gestalt therapy is conducted in the workshops. Workshops are scheduled for a finite period of time, some for as little as one day. Some are weekend workshops ranging from 10 to 20 or more hours, and others are more extended in duration. A typical workshop consists of one Gestalt therapist and 12 to 16 people treated over a weekend period. Given longer periods (ranging from a week to a month or longer) as many as 20 people can be seen by one therapist. Usually, however, if the group is larger than 16, there are co-therapists.

Since workshops have a finite life, there are just so many hours available to the participants. Usually, there is high motivation on the part of most participants to get into the "hot-seat," that is to be the focus of attention and to "work." Sometimes, rules are established so that no one can work a second time till each participant has had an opportunity to work once. At other times, no such rules are set. Thus, depending on a person's willingness, audacity, and drive, some people may get to work several times during a workshop.

Use of the "Hot-Seat" and Other Techniques

In a recent article, Levitsky and I have described in some detail the use of the "hot-seat" and other techniques used in Gestalt therapy. Many therapists follow Perls' lead in the use of the "hot-seat" technique and will explain this to the group at the outset. According to this method, an individual expresses to the therapist his interest in dealing with a particular problem. The focus is then on the extended interaction between patient and group leader ("I and Thou").

As therapist and patient work together occasions arise in which the patient is asked to carry out some particular exercise, e.g. "Could you repeat what you just said, but this time with your legs uncrossed?" or "Could you look directly at me as you say this?" The attitude with which these exercises are carried out is an important element. The patient is gradually educated and encouraged to undertake these exercises in the spirit of experiment. One cannot really know the outcome beforehand even though a specific hunch is being tested. The spirit of experiment is taken seriously and the question raised, "What did you discover?" This kind of discovery is a very potent form of learning (Levitsky and Simkin, 1972, p. 140).

Ethical Considerations

Gestalt therapists view people as having the capacity to cope with life. Rather than impose on their patients their own values or strictures on how to live, the Gestalt therapists are interested in having their patients/trainees discover for themselves what values fit their own way of looking at life. Thus, patients are asked to experiment, to examine, to pick and choose, and to taste before swallowing.

An underlying corollary to the above is my conviction that there is enough room in this world for everyone. I do not need to force my views on others or "justify my existence." I can usually find a subculture which shares my values if I do not accept or agree with the majority of values of the larger culture. In the extreme I can create my *own* subculture if need be.

The basic drive or energy in Gestalt therapy is oral aggression. Perls contended that this was necessary in order to be able to taste, and to discover what is nourishing and what is toxic. Then one can destructure the ideas, or food, or whatever, and assimilate, following tasting.

Based then on the assumption that the person can be self-regulatory, the Gestalt therapist encourages experimentation to discover what "fits." Naranjo (1971), in his article titled "Present Centeredness, Technique, Prescription and Ideal," says, "There are a number of implicit moral injunctions in Gestalt therapy," and he lists nine of these. He believes that these nine include living now, living here, stopping imagining, stopping unnecessary thinking, expressing, giving in to unpleasantness and pain, accepting no shoulds or oughts other than your own, taking full responsibility for one's own actions, feelings and thoughts, and surrendering to being who you are. He further indicates, although such injunctions as part of a moral philosophy are paradoxical to the point of view of Gestalt therapy which is anti-injunctions, the paradox is resolved when these points of view or injunctions are looked at as statements of "truth rather than duty" (p. 50).

I believe that the basic ethical attitude of the Gestalt therapist is that if you experiment you have the possibility of discovering what is suitable for you. If you swallow whole, there is no possibility of growth, no matter how potentially nourishing the food, idea, etc., may be. Most Gestalt therapists believe that the goal in Gestalt therapy *is* maturation and growth and that maturity, which Perls defines as "the transition from environmental support to self-support" can only be accomplished through the focusing of awareness and learning to discriminate what is useful for oneself.

One great immediate concern in terms of ethics is the ability of the Gestalt therapist. Shepherd points out that,

Since Gestalt techniques facilitate access to and release of intense affect, a therapist using this approach must neither be afraid nor inept in allowing the patient to follow through and finish the experience of grief, rage, fear, or joy. The capacity to live in the present and to offer solid presence standing by are essential. Without such presence and skill the therapist may leave the patient aborted, unfinished, opened, and vulnerable—out of touch with any base of support, either in himself or available from the therapist. The therapist's capacity for I—thou, here-and-now relationships is a basic requirement and is developed through extensive integration of learning and experience. Probably the most effective application of Gestalt techniques (or any other therapeutic techniques) comes with personal therapeutic experiences gained in professional training workshops and work with competent therapists and supervisors (Fagan and Shepherd, 1970, p. 238).

In addition, Shepherd points out the following as one of possible consequences of Gestalt therapy:

The consequences of successful Gestalt therapy may be that by teaching the patient to be more genuinely in touch with himself, he will experience more dissatisfaction with conventional goals and relationships, with the hypocrisy and pretense of much social interaction, and may experience the pain of seeing the deficiencies and destructiveness of many social and cultural forces and institutions. Simply stated, extensive experience with Gestalt therapy will likely make patients more unfit for or unadjusted to contemporary society (Fagan and Shepherd, 1970, p. 238).

Limitations of Gestalt Therapy

I consider Gestalt therapy as the treatment of choice for people who are "up in their head" most of the time. On the other hand, with people who are given to acting out, that is, who do not think through or do not fully experience their behavior, I would hesitate to use Gestalt therapy as a treatment of choice. A good rule of thumb is that for *experienced* therapists, Gestalt therapy is usually an effective tool if used with populations they feel comfortable with. Gestalt therapy has been used successfully with a wide range of populations including children, adolescents and adults.

For some Gestalt therapists the use of Gestalt therapy in groups is limiting. Shepherd maintains that the therapist may, by becoming too active, foster passivity of others in groups, while working with someone in the "hot-seat." Thus, facilitating the growth of one person may at the same time be

> . . . defeating his own goal of patient self-support. In this case, the group responds passively, regarding the therapist as an expert or magician, and themselves as having little to contribute without his special techniques and skill (Fagan and Shepherd, 1970, p. 23).

John Barnwell's work with ghetto adults in a poverty program (Simkin, 1968), and Janet Lederman's (1969) work with six- to ten-year-old behavioral problem children in the heart of an urban poverty area underline the point of view that the therapist or educator's competence with certain populations is much more important than the technique as such.

Suggested Readings

There has been a sharp increase in interest and the practice of Gestalt therapy during the past decade (1963–1973). At the time this chapter is being written (mid 1973) there are several Gestalt therapy institutes throughout the United States with at least three offering systematic training (Cleveland, San Francisco and Los Angeles).

Several books have appeared in the last three years ranging from a collection of ten older articles in *Festschrift for Fritz Perls* (Simkin, 1968) to the excellent collection of 25 articles in the book, *Gestalt Therapy Now,* focusing on theory, technique and application of Gestalt therapy by Fagan and Shepherd (1970).

Kogan (1970), concerned with the (then) absence of a systematic bibliography of source material in Gestalt therapy, collected and published a pamphlet which lists books, articles, papers, films, tapes, institutes and the *Gestalt Therapist Directory.* He includes approximately 90 references. Fagan and Shepherd list over 60 references. Yontef (1971) cites 45 references.

During 1972, two chapters dealing with Gestalt therapy appeared in two different books. In the Sager and Kaplan (1972) collection, Simkin's "The Use of Dreams in Gestalt Therapy" appeared under the "New Approaches" section, and in Solomon and Berzon's (1972) collection Levitsky and Simkin have a chapter dealing with the use of Gestalt therapy in small groups.

Perls' autobiographical book, *In and Out of the Garbage Pail* (1969), and Simkin's interview of him in 1966 give much of the historical background of the development of Gestalt therapy. Also of historical interest are the two excellent papers written by F. Perls' widow, Laura Perls (1953, 1956).

Practically none of the Gestalt therapy literature has been channeled through conventional sources during the three decades of its existence. Major exceptions are Fritz Perls' (1948) article in the *American Journal of Psychotherapy* and Polster's (1966) more recent article in *Psychotherapy.*

Until 1969, the only films depicting Gestalt therapy were all of F. Perls. His are still the primary sources (over 30 varied films) with one exception: Simkin's (1969) training film. Simkin now has his training film (1969) available on ½ inch video-tape as well as two later training video-tapes made in 1971 and 1973.

No Gestalt therapy library is considered complete
without the two basic books, *Gestalt Therapy* by Perls, Hefferline and Goodman (1951, 1965), and *Gestalt Therapy
Verbatim* by F. Perls (1969).

References

1. Barnwell, J. E., "Gestalt Methods and Techniques in a Poverty
   Program," in Simkin, J.S. (Ed.), *Festschrift for Fritz Perls.*
   Los Angeles: 1968.
2. Fagan, J., and Shepherd, I.L., *Gestalt Therapy Now.* Palo
   Alto, California: Science and Behavior Books, Inc., 1970.
3. Kogan, J., *Gestalt Therapy Resources.* San Francisco:
   Lodestar Press, 1970.
4. Lederman, J., *Anger and the Rocking Chair: Gestalt
   Awareness with Children.* New York: McGraw-Hill, 1969.
5. Levitsky, A., and Perls, F. S., in Fagan and Shepherd (Eds.),
   Gestalt Therapy Now. Palo Alto, California: Science and
   Behavior Books, Inc., 1970.
6. Levitsky A. and Simkin, J. S., in Solomon, L. N., and Berzon,
   B. (Eds.), *New Perspectives on Encounter Groups.* San Francisco: Jossey-Bass, Inc., 1972, pp. 245-254.
7. Naranjo, C., "Present Centeredness: Technique, Prescription
   and Ideal," in Fagan and Shepherd (Eds.), *Gestalt Therapy
   Now.* New York: Harper Colophon Books, 1971.
8. Perls, Laura, "Notes on the psychology of give and take,"
   Complex, 1953, *9,* 24–30.
9. Perls, Laura, "Two instances of Gestalt therapy," *Case
   Reports in Clinical Psychology.* Kings County Hospital,
   Brooklyn, New York, 1956.
10. Perls, F. S., *Ego, Hunger and Aggression.* London: Allen and
    Unwin, 1947; New York: Random House, 1969.
11. Perls, F. S., "Theory and technique of personality integra-
    tion," *American Journal of Psychotherapy,* 1948, 2, pp.
    565-586.
12. Perls, F. S., Hefferline, R. F., and Goodman, P., *Gestalt
    Therapy.* New York: Julian Press, 1951 (Republished: New
    York: Dell, 1965).

13. Perls, F. S., "Workshop vs. individual therapy," *Journal of the Long Island Consultation Center,* Vol. 5, No. 2 Fall, 1967, pp. 13–17.
14. Perls, F. S., *Gestalt Therapy Verbatim.* Lafayette, Calif.: Real People Press, 1969.
15. Perls, F. S., *In and Out of the Garbage Pail.* Lafayette, Calif.: Real People Press, 1969.
16. Polster, E., "A contemporary psychotherapy," *Psychotherapy: Theory, Research and practice,* 1966, *3,* pp. 1–6.
17. Pursglove, P. S., *Recognition in Gestalt Therapy.* New York: Funk and Wagnalls, 1968.
18. Sager, C. J., and Kaplan, H. S., (Eds.), *Progress in Group and Family Therapy.* New York: Brunner/Mazel, 1972.
19. Simkin, J. S., (Ed.), *Festschrift for Fritz Perls.* Los Angeles: Author, 1968.
20. Simkin, J. S., *Individual Gestalt Therapy: Interview with Dr. Frederick Perls.* Audio-tape recording. A.A.P. Tape Library, No. 31, Philadelphia, Pa.
21. Simkin, J. S., *In the Now.* A Training Film. Beverly Hills, Calif., 1969.
22. Simkin, J. S., in Sager, C. J., and Kaplan, H.S., (Eds.), *Progress in Group and Family Therapy.* New York: Brunner/Mazel, 1972, pp. 95–104.
23. Solomon, L.N., and Berzon, B., (Eds.), *New Perspectives on Encounter Groups.* San Francisco: Jossey-Bass, Inc., 1972.
24. Van Dusen, W., "Existential analytic psychotherapy," *American Journal of Psychoanalysis.* 1960, pp. 310–322.
25. Warren, Howard D., *Dictionary of Psychology.* New York: Houghton Mifflin & Co., 1934.
26. Yontef, G. M., *A Review of the Practice of Gestalt Therapy.* Trident Shop, California State College, Los Angeles, 1971.

Section II

Theoretical and
Practical Issues

On Awareness

J: Fritz used a very beautiful phrase, "Don't push the river; it flows by itself."

P: Is it one thing to have that on a "should" level and another thing to experience it as rhythm?

J: Yes. As soon as you change something into a "should," you are on a different trip. Any time you use awareness in the service of your top dog, what you are doing is using awareness to feed your top dog and you're not doing anything else at that moment. AWARENESS IS A TOOL and if you are aware, then you have choices. The more awareness you have, the more you can pick and choose; the more choices you can make. If you have more information or increased knowledge, you might make some other choice.

There is no "should" in the matter of awareness and I'm not saying that you "should" be aware at all. If you are unaware, you are unaware. If you make awareness a "should," then like any other "should," it becomes something that is no longer what you are doing; it's what you "should" be do-ing and becomes a very different kind of experience.

If I'm aware that I'm striving, that I'm trying hard, then that is what I am doing, and that's what I'm aware of. If I'm aware that I'm top-dogging myself then that is what I am do-ing. The moment that I switch from actual awareness to "shoulds" without being aware that I've gotten into the "should groove" then I lose awareness, become blinded. When I attend to what I am doing, that doesn't mean that I should change my posture, stop my computing, or whatever it is that I am doing. Awareness means that I have the possibility to change, as opposed to telling myself: "Aha, this is what you are doing, and you shouldn't be; you should be doing something else."

P: You said that awareness is needed for survival . . .

J: Awareness is needed for choices; without awareness you can't make choices. In some instances, it might also mean survival. To me, awareness has the value of my being able to choose. I prefer to choose. I feel more in control; not "controlling," but *IN* control. Master of my own destiny, running my own show, whatever terms you like. I'm making decisions either volitionally or or-ganismically, through awareness. And if I become aware that I am torturing myself, zapping into myself, I like knowing that I'm in control.

I have no way of controlling you. I can tell myself a story—the story is that if I manipulate you you'll go through the hoops, and I imagine then that I am con-trolling you. That is not accurate. What is accurate is that I manipulate you and if *you* are willing, then you go through the hoops. If you are not willing, then you play "spiteful," or "beartrap" or whatever.

I am discovering more and more that by being direct, saying openly what I want, I get much more. My payoff is greater than through indirectness, manipulation or emotional blackmail. I don't think there is anything intrinsically good or bad about being an emotional blackmailer, or not being one. The point is, do I get what I want by being direct or by being a manipulator or blackmailer? If I can get what I want by being direct, then that has value for me. If I can get more of what I want by being indirect, that's valuable. I experiment with discovering how I get more for myself. For me, the payoff is what counts. I'm able to get a bigger payoff by being direct. You may discover that you get more for yourself by being indirect. I'm asking you to consider experimenting with being direct, indirect, manipulating, not manipulating, in order to find out what gives you more for yourself. I don't think there's any great value in your emulating somebody else if it doesn't pay off for you.

Top-dog—Under-dog

J: I want to say something about the *top-dog under-dog concept.*

The theory is that the top-dog consists of all of the introjected, swallowed "shoulds" (how you should be in terms of values, ideas, way of being) which may or may not be how you would like to be now. The whole idea of top-dog means that you've swallowed whole, you've introjected something that didn't necessarily serve you at the time, but that you were forced by parent, teacher or whoever, to swallow. This includes whole ideas, attitudes, ways, etc. Top-dog consists of a number of these introjected whole ways of behavior which you still trot out, even though *here and now* that attitude, that way of behaving is no longer necessary, or even appropriate.

Then you also develop a counter-balancing force, the under-dog. The under-dog is the saboteur, the one that says, "Of course I will, tomorrow." It proclaims all kinds of declarations of intention and much of the

energy that is invested in "shoulding" yourself is dissi-
pated by the energy that is invested in sabotaging that
part of yourself.

If I examine my "should," e.g. "I *should* call my
parents," and explore for the moment the question,
"Do I *want* to call my parents?" I may find out that
calling them is something that makes sense to me, that I
want to do *here and now*. As soon as I take something
out of the "*should*istic" realm and put it into the
"*is*istic" realm (something that I want to do, that suits
me), then I have choices without wasting a lot of energy
in "should" and guilt. Do I want to? I don't know
whether I want to. O.K. If I don't know, I can experiment. Experimenting means risking and finding out. It
does not mean knowing the results beforehand. You
may find out, "It's still true—I don't want to call
them." It's no longer, "I *should* call them." I am
responsible as to whether or not to call.

There are various ways to deal with top-dog. One way
is to go with it and exaggerate it until the whole thing
becomes ridiculous. Another way is to follow it all the
way down the line and never question it. The most difficult way to deal with top-dog is to take a look at and
really examine each "should," *in the now*. After many
years of experience, however, my top-dog is often very
sneaky and knows how to give me a "should" without
my even being aware of it. So, if you have a bright
clever top-dog, "shouldism" is sometimes impossible to
deal with in the now since before you know it, your
top-dog has given you a "should" and you've acted on
it without awareness. The task of dealing with a bright
top-dog by yourself is very difficult. It is a moderately
easy task to deal with if you're working with a therapist
who reflects, "What you are doing now is . . ." He mir-
rors or makes you aware that you are top-dogging yourself at the moment. When you are working with yourself *and* you have a clever top-dog, then the other ways

are usually easier. One way is to exaggerate top-dog and become aware of how ridiculous, how out of line top-dog is, and you laugh him off stage. It depends on whether you can laugh at yourself. If you are the kind of person who takes yourself very seriously, this technique won't work. It will work if you have a sense of humor, a sense of your own ludicrousness. There is something a bit bizarre about all human behavior, including my own. I can laugh at myself if I become aware that I am acting on a "should," as if my top-dog really knows what is best for me. It is as if whoever gave me all these "shoulds" (parents, teachers, etc.) were brighter than I and knew more than I do about what is right for me. *I* am the *only person* who really knows what's right for me. So at any time something that is *not me* begins to nudge, I'm very skeptical. Sometimes I can deal with my top-dog by ridicule.

Another way to work with top-dog is to play *perfectionist,* to do everything your top-dog demands and never question. If you do this, what may happen is that you and your top-dog become one and so there is no more top-dog. You really become the "should" self and so there is no longer the top-dog under-dog game. You always do what your top-dog says: you're always the boy scout. Mr. Clean, the all-American boy. Then you have no more problems with top-dog.

P: But doesn't he make more and more demands? Doesn't he become even more top-doggish?

J: No, as soon as top-dog becomes part of your morality, ethics, life style, there are no more demands. It is no longer an introject; it becomes part of what is right for you. So, if the top-dog says "you *should* keep appointments" and the under-dog says "no," then there is a struggle going on. However, if I go with top-dog and follow it and if this suits me, there is no longer a struggle. I now keep appointments without even questioning—this has become part of me, part of my way. It is no longer a foreign object I've swallowed whole, no longer an introject. I like to experiment. For years I imagined that I had to set an alarm clock since I "should" get up, but I didn't want to. I worked on a job that I hated and I wouldn't let myself be aware of how much I hated it. Now, I have no difficulty in getting up at a given time or keeping an appointment. I'm not forcing myself to do it; it is something that I want to do. Another thing I discovered is that when I used to get myself lost driving somewhere, I had the rationale, "I have a bad sense of direction," which is true and also bullshit. Now when I get myself lost, my message to me is very clear: "Jim, you don't want to go there and you're pushing yourself to go there." At that point I have a choice: I can acknowledge that I don't want to go there and I'm pushing myself to go; then I can decide if that is what I want. I'm not suggesting that I give up judging or programming. I am suggesting using my awareness to know where I am at that moment and then do what I feel is right for me. Sometimes I will go where I don't want to go. I push myself or choke myself into going somewhere. I still don't always listen.

I feel very good when I fulfill contracts. I've experimented with not fulfilling contracts and I feel very bad. So, what suits me is to be responsible, to assume obligations. What I have learned about me is that I won't obligate myself to do things that I already know I don't like. I will not accept invitations to big cocktail parties—I hate them. I will not go to meetings or bore myself by sitting on committees. These are activities that I don't like. I don't obligate myself, sign contracts for things I don't like to say, "No," to begin with if some chick says, "Let's ball," and I don't feel any excitement or interest and I start to tell myself, "She'll feel bad," or "I should" or anything like that. That's bullshit. If I don't feel any excitement or interest that's where I am, and I say, "No."

P: You make the contract for those things that you know fit you and therefore you can be responsible for?

J: That I imagine I will be response-able for.

P: Jim, I have a hang-up with the practical aspect of doing what I want to do. For example, if a client comes in and I don't feel like seeing him, sometimes I will say "I don't want to work with you." However, then my income starts to decrease and I feel concerned about that.

J: For me, it's just the reverse. The more I say, "No," the more the phone rings, the more offers I get. I have no trouble about income. It's a matter of selecting who I want to work with and where I want to work. By saying, "No," there's more pounding at my door.

Should versus Is

J: I want to talk about the process of staying with what is. The whole process of being, for me, has this at the core. If what is happening is that I'm in my head making up theories, that's what is at the moment. If I'm listening to you or looking at the sunset, that's what is. This is what is foreground for me at the moment. Most processes which are ongoing become background if I insist on some other process being foreground. Most of the time I have the choice: *I* decide, I form another Gestalt which is the foregound, and then, whatever the other process was—pain, pleasure, work, thinking,— becomes background as I choose the new process. What is difficult for me and I imagine for you, is to stay with my awareness, to stay with what I am doing from moment to moment, i.e. to stay in touch with what *is.* What often happens is that "what is" becomes "what should be." (I should be writing now instead of looking at the sunset; I should be listening more carefully to you; I should be more feeling; etc.) Even "I should be" staying with the awareness continuum (and I'm not).

What I am doing at this point is top-dogging myself, "shoulding" myself. I lose awareness at this point and get into the "I shouldn't" swamp.

P: Is pushing yourself the same as "should"? For example, pushing yourself to grow?

J: Any pushing is not accepting how I am, saying that I should be different from what I am, not staying with what *is.* This is fruitless, since at any given moment I can't be different from how I am.

There are various possibilities for change. The simplest is staying aware of how I am, remaining in touch with myself. Sometimes change comes automatically, without any programming or willingness. However, sometimes awareness alone is not enough to produce change. Once I become aware of how I go against myself, I can begin to program change. I can begin to program something else. I can experiment with other forms of behavior.

The Five Layers of You

We often hear the statement, "There is nothing much to him underneath the surface." The surface is one of about five layers of personality. The surface layer is the so-called "polite layer," a "sentence layer"—sentences like, "Good morning," "How are you?" "Nice to see you," "Been to Lake Tahoe before?" "What do you do for a living?" We all have a stock of these sentences for that kind of sentence-throwing.

If I get beyond the sentence-throwing layer, there's the role-playing layer—role-playing as a shrink or role-playing as a professor, father, male. I have certain roles and certain ways of coming on in these roles that are prescribed, routine, acceptable, organized roles. But again, *I* am not there; my *role* is there, my way of coming on is there. Sometimes two people make contact this way. One role meets another role. You go downtown to the casinos and there are these dealers with their wooden faces; that's their role-playing and my role-playing is as a sucker or gambler and the two roles meet. It's a little bit like the analyst who has a little secret door that he can sneak out of when his patient is on the couch free-associating—he has a tape-recorder going. There's a bar about two doors away and he goes there and has a couple of martinis. He's back in his seat just before the hour is up and he's sitting there when the patient gets off the couch. One day he's out having his usual martini or two and there's his goddam patient! He says, "What the hell are you doing here? You're supposed to be on the couch free-associating!" Patient says, "I got myself a tape-recorder and I recorded my session and now my tape-recorder is talking to your tape-recorder."

Sometimes, if I'm willing to give up my polite games, my sentences, my role-playing, I come to a feeling of emptiness, nothingness, no-thingness in the Zen sense, and this is very frightening—to be empty, to imagine that all there is to me are sentences and games, role-playing—and that's it! Most people, when they reach the role-playing level of personality are unwilling to go beyond that. Some people do get beyond their role-playing; they get to their empty spot, their nothingness spot, and they are not willing to go beyond that, or they imagine that there is nothing beyond that. However, beyond the emptiness, the blankness, is the implosive-explosive layer.

The implosive layer is sometimes called the dead layer and explosive layer is sometimes called the hysterical layer. Essentially the explosive layer is what you are talking about doing when you say that your emotions are right at the surface—that you're ready to cry, you're ready to laugh or you're ready to explode into some strong feeling. For example, strong sexual feeling is exploded into orgasm. In an interpersonal social situation you might be exploding into anger or into joy, fury or tears.

The explosiveness is frequently pushed down, especially in certain societies, certain subcultures, and so the *ex*plosiveness becomes *im*plosiveness, a squeezing, a holding-on, and is characterized by psychosomatic disturbances such as ulcers, migraine—all kinds of very unpleasant bodily sicknesses for which the physicians can find no organic cause. Beneath all of this nonsense if *you,* and you are explosive. You are whatever you are and as soon as you swallow the idea, "You have no right to be you," all the other spurious layers are activated. You are who you are and when somebody disapproves and tells you, "You shouldn't be who you are," then you take on these other outer layers which are phoney—for you. If you are a quiet, peaceful sort of person, perhaps you've been told you *should* be more alive, or you *should* be more animated, or you *should* be more friendly. If you are an outgoing sort of person and have been told that you *should* be quieter, withdrawn, or whatever—these *shoulds* get in the way.

There is no prescribed way to be. There is no "adjusted" way to be. The way to be is to be you—whoever you are. If you swallow in the beginning the lie that there is no room in this world for you *the way you are,* then you're stuck with having to play a phoney game the rest of your life. And that lie, I think, is the most immoral lie of all—whether it is laid on you by a parent, or a theologian, or whoever. You have a right to be in this world the way you are; there is *plenty of room in the world for everybody.*

On Self-Expression

J: I want to talk about expressing myself and how I interfere with my self-expression. Sometimes I stop myself from expressing myself because of my fear of how the other person will react. For example, I may get angry and express some of my anger, but then become afraid that if I continue to be angry people will retaliate and hurt me or fight back. If that happens, I interfere with my anger and stay with my fantasy of what's going to happen. I believe that then I depress myself and retroflect my anger at that point. [To participant:] What I'm imagining is that you become aware that you are expressing yourself, then you stop yourself before you have fully expressed. The rest of your anger you experience as retroflected depression. When I allow my rage out completely the feedback I get is nowhere near what I had imagined. As a matter of fact sometimes the other person feels very relieved. As my wife says, "Now I can live with you again!"

P: Are there only two alternatives? Either keeping your anger in or letting it out?

J: Yes. Once a feeling starts, it has to go somewhere. I can tell myself the story that I don't have the feeling, but that doesn't change the fact that the feeling is there. It can either go outside toward someone else, or it gets retroflected in me. The stories that I tell myself or that I've been told say, "control yourself," "squeeze yourself." If I do that I find that the feeling stays inside me, gets retroflected, and I don't express myself.

P: How does that fit with the idea of early feelings, feelings that are unfinished and therefore still going on?

J: When the anger in the original situation is unfinished, what happens is that I become the recipient of my own anger and it is still not out here, where it belongs. That may be enough to satisfy me at the moment. If I dig a deep enough ulcer or whatever I'm doing to me, that might take care of the feeling at the moment. But it isn't enough and I'm still unfinished. When a feeling is fully expressed and the target is the right target, then there is the Gestalt, the completion.

P: That puts it all together for me.

P2: If you are angry at someone else and you merely express that to him verbally, is that enough, or is this something that has to come out more dramatically?

J: I don't understand the difference. If I say to someone that I'm angry with him that may be enough. It's enough if I feel finished. I can scare myself by imagining that I have to go out and butcher somebody to express myself fully. Well, that means lots and lots of pent up feelings that I have not released. But, when I finally do express my rage, I don't butcher anybody. If I don't handle my feelings openly, I have the potential of becoming a killer. You know the very sweet gentle ones you read about in the headlines every once in a while; the model boy who's gone to church for 17 years. He's the type who has squeezed himself in for a long time, and finally does explode and commit murder.

P: Is your feeling of being relieved of the anger related to how the other person responds to it? For example, she [participant] got angry at you just now and expressed it. Whether or not you actually felt hurt or insulted by it is another question. The important thing is that she expressed her feelings.

J: Yes. And that brings up another issue which to me is a core issue relating to self-expression. I believe that the function of self-expression is to express myself. I'm not convinced that the function of self-expression is to influence, change, reform, the other. It *may* happen, that in expressing myself I influence the other person. But if I believe that the *function* of self-expression is to influence the other, then each time I express myself and the other one just doesn't care, I feel more and more frustrated and impotent.

P: You feel you just can't get through to him.

J: That feeling is based on the false assumption that self-expression is to influence others and that is not true. The only person I can influence and only after working quite hard, is me. The influencing of others has to do with their cooperation, with their willingness to be intimidated. If someone is not willing, then I may experience impotence . . . if I believe I have the power to influence others.

On Taking Responsibility

J: For me, the most difficult task of all is to take full responsibility for what I do and what I say. Also to stay aware of all of the games I have, the ways of dissimulating, of being unaware. It is easy enough for me to focus my attention on you. And easy, I imagine, for some of you to focus your attention on whoever is on the hot-seat—thus losing touch with *yourself* and *being responsible for you.*

What I'm responsible for at this moment is my lecturing, my talking about responsibility. I'm also responsible for checking myself, for watching my little truth button down here [referring to crossed ankles] to see if I *do* become aware of when I do this. What I was aware of just then was my voice fading out and I'm responsible for that.

One of my non-constructive games is what I call "awareness in the service of the top-dog." Instead of just realizing that this *is* what I'm doing—I *am* fading out, or I *am* crossing my ankles and accepting this behavior as a simple fact, I use my awareness to put myself down. Then my attitude is, "Aha! Your ankles are crossed! Aha! Your voice is fading out!" This is a very intricate and subtle process and it takes a lot of practice to get it straightened out. My top-dog is very tricky, very sneaky and I have to be on the alert to make sure that I don't use my awareness against myself.

I am using this situation to learn more about me. I hope that you use this situation to learn more about you as well as whoever is in the hot-seat. It is so easy to get intrigued and fascinated with someone else and to get away from self-awareness.

I'm not saying that you *shouldn't* do this; I'm asking you, if you can, to stay with your awareness, to be aware that this *is* what you are doing, that you are using whoever is here to distract yourself. "What I am doing now is distracting myself" or "I'm listening." Acknowledge that without any judgment. For me that is extremely difficult. I *can* do that more as I stay aware. I imagine that you can do this more as you stay more aware, especially if you become aware that you are using awareness to feed your top-dog, to beat yourself. For me, that is the most difficult work for me to do—to walk this thin line.

P: Jim, I wonder if you would say a few words about the difference between "I feel" and "I believe."

J: Some of you have been trained to say "I feel" when you believe something. Unfortunately, this is a sloppiness which is built into our language and which often blurs the distinctions between *feel, believe, think, imagine,* etc. It is important in our work to make clear distinctions in the use of these words, particularly since we find it so basic to distinguish between feelings and emotions on the one hand and head-tripping on the other.

"I feel . . ." is for "I feel angry . . . curious . . . bad."

"I believe" equals "I have a conviction."

"I think" is what I am doing when I am computing.

"I imagine" is when I'm using my computer to fantasize.

Feelings are feelings; thoughts are thoughts; fantasies are fantasies! These are not mere semantic differences; they have basic implications for our work. This is an issue of responsibility. Responsibility for language.

In the film *Gone With The Wind* there is a beautiful sequence in which the whistle blows while the slaves are working and somebody says, "Quittin' time!" The foreman says, "Who says it's quittin' time? I'll say when it's quittin' time. QUITTIN' TIME!" He's saying, "I'll decide. I'm running the show!" He's taking responsibility.

Self-Support and Environmental Support

J: I want to talk a little about the issue of self-support and environmental support. For Fritz Perls, the ideal of self-support was very important: for a person to be able to stand entirely on his own two feet. However, I don't believe it's possible for me or you to live in the world without experiencing interdependency needs. I don't believe that to be completely self-supportive is ideal; I think that's a blind spot that Fritz had. However, I believe that in Fritz' last few years he became more aware of this with his dream of a kibbutz where each person shared responsibility and was interdependent with others. I believe that there is a balance between self-support and utilizing the support of others. What the balance is, each person must decide for himself.

If I can stand on my own two feet, if I am able to do for myself, then I feel good; I feel comfortable with being able to do something. I also feel good when I can mobilize somebody else to do something that I can't do, won't do, or do badly. Where I've learned to manipulate or mobilize other people to take care of me, to do things for me, I cripple myself intentionally or unintentionally by not learning that I can do this for myself. It doesn't mean that I *have to* or that I necessarily *want to*. What I do want to find out is whether or not I am *able* to. For example, for many years I never changed a tire on my car. I always had somebody do it for me. I didn't know whether I was capable of doing it, whether I would like it or not. Recently I changed a tire and know that I *can* if I have to and I find that I prefer not to. I find that I now have the choice. By allowing myself to discover what I can do or can't do, will or won't do, I have many more possibilities, many more avenues. If I don't do this, I may be so identified with my environmental supports (money, social role, children, etc.) that I may imagine that I can't exist when I don't have these supports. I may prefer to have them, but I know that I can survive without them. When I know through experimenting that I can't fix or change or repair or whatever, then I know I have to have a plumber or electrician or mechanic. I know I've attempted the task and it's not my thing. If I've attempted and found that I could do it, I feel "wow," this is something I really enjoy. I sometimes discover that I've cheated myself all these years by telling myself the story that I *can't* do something. Actually, it is that I won't and I haven't experimented to find out.

So, I'm putting in a plug for some kind of balance between self-support and environmental support. I don't know what balance is right for you. This you have to discover for yourself—again, through experimenting, through *doing,* rather than thinking about, talking about or imagining.

On Contracts

J: There are two kinds of contracts. One is a contract which is called a non-negotiable contract, meaning a contract which is forever and ever. In essence, most people by not killing themselves are agreeing to live, to remain alive. Once you kill yourself, that's a highly non-negotiable contract.

The kind of contracts that I like and that I would recommend especially in marriages, are contracts that you renegotiate, preferably every day. Or if you don't see each other every day, or you aren't talking every day, at least renegotiate your contract each week. The marriage contract that has not been renegotiated for several weeks is, I think, a very sterile contract. If it hasn't been renegotiated for several months, it's probably a dead one, and I think that any kind of contract that's non-negotiable guarantees some kind of deadness.

If I were a dictator, I would make sure that all contracts were written with negotiation clauses added, to renegotiate, to reopen negotiations at any time. I would have the requirement, that they be reexamined, looked at again, even if it is just to say, "O.K., I'm still willing," on the part of *both* parties. Examples are the government and the aerospace industry, the soldier and the military, the husband and the wife, the parent and the kid. Let them both say, "O.K., I'm still willing."

In some situations, the person who has the *power* is not willing *at all* to write an open contract. He only wants one kind of contract—one where he keeps the power. If the person who has the power writes that kind of contract, that's it! There's no choice. The kid can't write a negotiable contract, the parent can. The person with the power is the only one who can write a negotiable contract. If the white in the white-black struggle writes a non-negotiable contract, that's it! The only possibility is to revolt and, as in the military, those become revolutionary situations. Where there is goodwill in contract writing and the willingness to negotiate, I would urge the considering of renegotiating clauses.

P: Could you illustrate what you mean? Say between a husband and wife?

J: Sure. Sit down and talk with your wife and say, "Hey, I'm no longer willing." If your contract is to obey then, "I'm no longer willing to obey. I promised I would cherish. I'm not cherishing you and I don't want to make that kind of promise any more. That's not where I am." Whatever your agreement was, if it's not true now, and you know it's not true now, *then* if you keep playing a game *as if* you are still obeying or cherishing or whatever the agreement is, that is *nonsense.* You're living a lie; you're playing a game.

P: Then you shouldn't take the vows in the first place, if they are all so one-sided, and they don't consider the other.

J: Well, you made an agreement at that time. That is what felt right for you, O.K.

P: But you're talking about twenty years later, aren't you? You keep coming back to the same thing. I'm feeling sort of stupid. I'm just beginning to realize [slowly]. You come back with the same thing *all the time* and in all circumstances and what I understand is that if it doesn't fit, if it doesn't make you feel right, it isn't right.

J: You are *not* stupid, and really, that's the message. If you're willing to live a lie, to make yourself uncomfortable, to give yourself a headache or ulcers or whatever, and if you like playing a martyr—great! Only don't pin that on the other. That's where *you* are. You enjoy hurting yourself, you enjoy playing martyr, being Mr. Nice Guy and always being grabbed by the short hair. That's your thing. Where you and I have really boxed ourselves in is when *we* imagine: "Hey! *You're* choking me!" *You* are choking yourself again. O.K. [to patient.] What don't you believe?

P: Well . . . .

J: Come on, you just choked yourself with something that you can't believe.

P: That's too one-sided. If I choke myself, it's an accident. [Laughter]

J: Nah! You choked yourself as you were saying, "I'm

playing brain damaged; I don't even know what I was saying."

P: Where I box myself in is when . . . . Wait!

J: O.K. I don't imagine. I know. I was playing then. I wasn't willing to be arrogant, but I *am* arrogant and that's where the trouble is.

There is lots of room in this world, enough for you and for me and everybody else. Sometimes I don't believe what I've said. Sometimes I don't believe that there is enough room in this world for everybody, and especially for me. I have to play a certain role or a certain game. And that's bullshit! To say that there aren't other people who might suit me—there's only *a* person who would suit me—is nonsense. I prefer certain people and there are people who suit me. And where I delude myself is by pretending that nobody else could possibly suit me, or that there is nobody else in the world who can do for me. That's not true! I scare myself with imagining that nobody else will suit me.

P: I know I have carried that over into what I do, too. Geology is the only thing I will ever enjoy doing. There are no alternatives. If I can't do that, I think, "What am I going to do? I'll die!"

P2: Yeah. I do that with skiing and that's really got to be a pain. It was just too much trying to make it into something that it wasn't. It wasn't easy; it wasn't relaxing; it wasn't warm all of the time.

J: Yeah. That's another thing I would do if I were dictator. I would make people change jobs, go into a whole different scene every X number of months or years.

[Following individual work with another participant wishing to terminate a relationship.]

J: The promissory note, the extracting of a promise, is

needed only when there is some queston. The business of obligating yourself is needed when you don't trust. I have a cousin who likes me a great deal, I like him a great deal, and we were building this house. He said if I needed money to call him. And so I did. I wrote him a long letter with details of the business thing, etc., and he wrote back and said, "I really don't want that kind of thing. Here's $25,000 and when you're finished with it, you can give it back to me."

He doesn't want a business transaction. He does a lot of business, millions of dollars, with all kinds of legal arrangements. In interpersonal things he doesn't want any of that. He's a very straight guy, and he experiences me as a very straight guy. I think if two people trust each other, they don't have to insist on documents, on promissory notes. If you give somebody dough and he's a crook, he's a crook, whether you have a promissory note or not. The whole promising bit is vengeful. It doesn't augur well for a relationship, to have to have all kinds of declarations of promises.

I believe you would do well to rewrite some of your contracts, so that you don't feel enslaved. I imagine that your alternatives are to be enslaved or to be completely independent. I think that you get yourself into trouble when you begin to relate to somebody and you imagine that the way you "should" relate is in this kind of enslaved, obedient way. It's the "Good Wife," or the "Good Daughter" or whatever you do. This is a game, and it isn't you. You scare yourself. You imagine you shouldn't be scared, and you are. And you want to run away. So you keep going through extremes. One extreme is being all by yourself, lonely, not answering the phone, etc.; and the other extreme is being confluent with someone, not feeling right about that.

I think that it is important to have the kind of relationship that you will feel most comfortable in: a position where you can have your own independence, your own pad, and you can come and go, stay, not stay, so that when you come in and unpack your things, the contract is, "I am here now and I am unpacking my things." That's what your commitment is. I think that you scare yourself by imagining that a contract has to be forever, or for a long period of time. To be aware that at any given moment you can split or stay, makes you aware of the thing that you are avoiding all the time. From moment to moment you have a choice. And that's what the whole thing is about—choosing.

The ultimate choice is the most scary one—that you have the choice of living or dying. You can choose to live or you can choose to kill yourself. This is your choice at any moment, to live or to die. Or you can torture yourself at any moment. You *do* have these choices. You have existential choices. What you are choosing to do when you are scaring yourself is, you are choosing to scare yourself, or to keep yourself tied down. What you are choosing to do when you walk out is to walk out. And it is not forever. That's the point. The getting out or coming back, the coming or going, is for the moment. The only thing that is forever, of course, is to kill yourself. Unless you have some inside resurrection hope, that's it! But the other things are not forever-and-ever things at all. Even though you might pretend that they are.

Shame and Disgust

J: There are two built-in organismic barriers which allow a person to live in this world with other people. One is shame; the other is disgust. If I do something that doesn't fit me, doesn't suit me, I will experience shame: an intense feeling of heat, embarrassment. That feeling is so intense that I will avoid the same behavior again because I don't like that intense feeling. The same is true of disgust. If I do something which is anti-organismic, if I do something which I'm totally disgusted with, I might even vomit. I feel that I can't swallow, I can't take that in, so I will avoid that situation, that behavior that disgusts me.

I have all the equipment I need to function in˙ the world. My organismic barriers of shame and disgust are enough. However along come people who say, "No, it's not true. You were born bad, you're born with original sin and to become civilized we have to add guilt." So the way they teach you to be civilized is to pile guilt on top of your shame and disgust. Many aspects of our culture involve making somebody feel inadequate, guilty, etc. Look at some of the phrases commonly used like "you ought to be ashamed of yourself." Well, if a person *is* ashamed he *is* ashamed. If you drag in "ought to," you're promoting guilt, not shame.

Resentment and Guilt

When I experience a resentment, I have a demand I have not made explicit. When I resent something in you, my demand is that you change, that you be different. If I have a resentment and I don't express the demand, (if my resentment doesn't go anywhere) I may retroflect it, turn it back against myself and feel guilty, since guilt is retroflected resentment or anger. It is anger that belongs out there, but is expressed in here, in the self. Once I've expressed my demand, my anger, then the guilt is gone. Guilt is man-made. It is not organismic. You can blame religion, or parents or whoever you feel is to blame for it. We have all been given the story that we should not voice our resentments or anger, but should turn those feelings against ourselves, i.e. feel guilty.

Polarities and Integration

[Participant has been working on arrogance versus humility.]

J: I want to add one thing that I haven't said before but I have implied. There are two sides to every coin. There are two sides to you. Polarities are the two sides to your coin. If you are aware of beating yourself and you identify with the beaten part, that's your side of the coin. Or, you may be aware of beating, but not in touch with the part of you that is being beaten. If you are aware of a part of you which feels put down, there is also a part of you which is doing the putting down. If you are a meek, humble guy, the other side is usually the arrogant, omnipotent guy. By getting in touch with both sides of the polarity, especially the side that you don't ordinarily identify with, there is the possibility of integration, of putting yourself together. To achieve integration, centeredness, and balance, you need to learn the two sides of your coin.

Attention

J: I'd like to coattail your work for a few minutes on the topic of attention. I'm convinced that I need attention, and I imagine that each of you needs attention. In my experience there isn't a single person who doesn't want and need as much attention as he can get. The problem is the ways in which we have learned to get attention. Some ways have been applauded and some have been put down. The basic need of being attended to is something we have no control over and need not control. The question is not whether or not I should get attention but rather *how* do I get the attention I need and want. What kind of attention fits for me? I foul myself up when I believe the story I've been taught that I "shouldn't" want or need to be attended to. In that event the business of guilt and "I shouldn't" comes into play.

Now if you get in touch with your need and attempt to put it down, you're in a box. The box is that you have a need, it's there, and there is nothing you can do except satisfy that need. If you attempt to deny it, or gloss it over, it will come out anyway. So, the issue is, "How do I get my needs attended to?" Once I become aware of what my needs are then I can choose how to express them. I'm "in control." I can ask the question, how can I be attended to in a way that I like? I suggest that you observe how other people have their needs attended to. See if you can learn techniques that you like, ways of being attended to that you like, that fit you. Usually in a group this size you'll find at least one way that you like and that you haven't attempted or experimented with before.

Emotional Blackmail

Some of you may not be familiar with how to play the emotional blackmail game. It's such a beautiful game and it's played so often that I'd like to make sure you know how to play.

First of all, you have to be clear about the basic rule. The basic rule is that in an interaction with another person, both of you are supposed to have similar reactions; if not, then one or both of you is supposed to feel bad in some way. For instance, if you do something nice and he doesn't, he agrees to feel guilty. If you have a pleasant experience—an orgasm, for instance—and the other doesn't, then you play *your* part by feeling guilty. It doesn't matter what the specific is—you act nice to someone and he doesn't respond. There you are.

Either or both of you has to agree that he will feel guilty if he doesn't reciprocate and even the score.

Once you have that kind of agreement, you have all the ingredients necessary for a nice game of emotional blackmail—and away you go!!!

My Needs and the Needs of Others

J: Father is taking his nine-year-old son to school, and there are two dogs, one mounted on top of the other. The little boy says, "Daddy, what are those two dogs doing?" "Well, son, the dog that's on top has hurt his front paws and the one that is underneath is helping him walk." The boy gets out and starts to walk toward school, then turns to his father and says, "You know, Daddy, that must be true of life in general. The minute you start being helpful, you get fucked!"

One way of being in this world is to be a megalomaniac, to imagine that nobody has power in this world except me. If I take what I want, if I suck, or if I am cruel, I imagine the other person has no choice—he has to comply. If I'm a sadist, he has to be the masochist; if I'm powerful, he has to be weak. This assumes that no one else in the world has a say—only I do. I can say what I want, do what I want, everybody else is passively there to serve me. In my head I can keep myself deluded this way and imagine that I shouldn't be powerful or that I shouldn't be cruel because the other people will crumble.

When I actually risk finding out what the world is all about, I find, "Yeah, there are some people who will suck when I play Universal Tit." If I want to play Universal Tit and they want to suck, we form a team, a balance in the social field. I'm the Universal Tit, they're the suckers, and we are both satisfied. Or conversely, I want to suck and somebody wants to be Universal Tit, then there's a balance.

I also discover, when I'm willing to risk, that when I go on being a bully, there may be somebody who is NOT willing to be bullied. He has power and strength and can say, "No" or "I don't want to." By experimenting with being who I am, I discover that I am not the only person in this world; more than that I'm not the only person in this world who has power or strength or who sucks or feeds.

When two people meet and their needs dovetail, then there's balance; if I have a need to be a dictator and someone else has a need to be a dictatee, then good—we make a balance. I can scare myself by surrounding myself very carefully with only dictatees when I play dictator, and then say, "The world consists of weak people who want to be told what to do." The converse is, if I like to be the dictatee, I can surround myself with only dictators. Then I can scare myself and say, "The world has only people who want to dictate, who want to whip me or beat me." This is not true, this is a way of very carefully selecting my world, of cutting out every other possibility and reinforcing my own head-trip. Actually, when I see and experience other people's strengths, their weaknesses, their desires, I find that there are lots of different kinds of people. Some of us work very well together. Some of us are poison for each other; we are not nourishing to each other. We don't form a balance.

And that is what is. As long as I stay inside of my head, make up stories, my world stays the same inside my head. I keep deluding myself, telling myself the same story, reinforcing, digging my rut deeper and deeper. The only way I know to find out about myself is by risking, not by having someone give me a guarantee card. If I get too scared, I can withdraw. That's O.K., as long as I am aware that that is what I am doing.

On Making Assumptions

[This follows an encounter with a patient which resulted in Dr. Simkin's drowsing off to sleep during the work.]

P: I get the feeling that there is never a time that one can speak to oneself in the hot-seat. Somehow it is not acceptable unless one directs it to you or to the group. I thought she was really talking to parts of herself and that's when you did your yawning and closed your eyes to show that you didn't exist for her.

J: What I believe is that anytime she wants to talk to part of herself, that's alright. What I object to is when this isn't clear and direct. If somebody says to me, "I want to leave you now and talk to part of me," and makes this explicit—that his interest at the moment is to make contact with part of himself, I'm very willing for him to work with part of himself. To be a captive audience is a manipulation that I object to. At any time that a person is explicit and says what he wants and what he is doing, I'm willing. I am not a mind reader. I have no degree in mind reading. And I don't know what's going on inside of your skin. Most of the difficulties I get into with people that I work with are when I *assume*—when I read their mind. I recently have coined a phrase: At the point where I give up my crystal balls, I re-own my own balls. I recommend this to those of you who have them or want them. [Laughter]

P2: Jim, when you said, "I imagine that this is a rehearsal" and you checked it out with her, and she said she never said this before, what do you think then?—that she wasn't ready for what you were saying?

J: My fantasy was wrong. I believed her when she said that she had never done this before and my crystal ball was defective.

P2: In other words, even when you check it out with a patient and he says, "No," it could be that you are on to something but he is not ready for it yet?

J: Yeah.

P2: How do you differentiate?

J: As much as I can, I stay with where the person is. If a person isn't there, he isn't there, whether it's his unconscious, up, down, sideways; if he isn't there, he isn't there.

P2:   Mmmhmmm.

J: To me, it makes no difference what the motive is; what matters is what the phenomenology is, what's happening, and what is happening *is* that the person isn't there.

On the Addictive Personality

J: Each of you knows how difficult it is to work with the addicted personality—the alcoholic, the person that's addicted to drugs. I consider mind-fucking an addiction now. Some people that I work with, I am convinced, are addicted mind-fuckers, and so the problem there is to become aware of the starting of the process and deliberately avoid the first mind fuck. I don't know whether after a period of stopping mind-fucking, whether one can go back. I don't have any clinical evidence. I *do* have clinical evidence that the prohibition, the treating of mind-fucking as an addiction, is effective with people that are willing to be aware when they start.

This means, of course, facing whatever this replaces, usually the emptiness, the staying with the nothingness. We each have a way of avoiding (*a*-voiding) voids. If I am prevented from role-playing or working my ass off or smoking, and if I can tolerate the withdrawal pain of not overworking or smoking, then I have a chance to face and work through the empty layer and become more real and more aware of my true potentials.

Breathing and Anxiety

J: I don't know if any of you are familiar with the

definition of anxiety as excitement without adequate support of oxygen. As one allows himself to feel more and more excited, he needs more and more oxygen for his excitement. Regardless of where your excitement is, whether the excitement is anger or joy or grief or sexual, you need air to support your excitement. For you [to participant] cutting off is right here [throat], other people do their cutting off over here [chest], or other places. Anxiety equals excitement minus sufficient support of oxygen. If you are anxious and you don't know what the excitement is, at least breathe! If you do this [taking a deep breath] you will become less anxious.

About Hanging On

J: There are two ways to go in dealing with "hanging on"—I call it the "hanging-on bite." When you clench your jaw, when I clench my jaw, nothing can get in, nothing can get out. Nothing happens other than my being defiant. I am not allowing any nurturing.

Now, sometimes when I become aware of clenching, my immediate top-dog thing is to say, "Uh, uh—stop clenching! You shouldn't clench!" and I prematurely let go before I've finished clenching. One way to deal with clenching is to finish, complete the situation, to keep clenching until you get tired of it. Then you are ready to let go. That is contrary to the usual way of interfering by saying, "Oh, I'm clenching and I shouldn't be," and not finishing. Even though you don't understand what your clenching is about, what your need is, it's a good idea to go with the clenching: *to finish is a way of letting go.* The usual tendency is to interfere and do something. Unclench. This may be premature and the clenching doesn't get finished, nor does the unclenching. This is not the *only* way. This is *a* way.

P: This session—was this primarily Gestalt therapy? I have a feeling that this was less Gestalt therapy and more of a psychotherapy session, with some aspects of encounter group worked in.

J: I don't have that clear an image of what is encounter work, what is psychotherapy, what is Gestalt therapy—those are all categories that I can't differentiate. I'm remembering now when I once did a demonstration for a group of hypnotherapists, their comment was, "But what you're doing is hypnotherapy."

Enough Room

This has to do with something that I said earlier that I want to elaborate on: the issue of there being enough room in this world for everybody.

At some point in my life, I was told, "You don't have the right to exist the way you are; in order to live in this world you have to change. This world will not accommodate you the way you are."

That was the first lie that I introjected; I swallowed it whole and I believed for over forty years that that was true, that there wasn't enough room in this world for me the way I was. I had to change myself, accommodate myself to how the world is, in terms of how somebody else saw the world and interpreted it to me.

This lie has been perpetuated and handed down from generation to generation, and some people began to question very seriously whether this lie has any validity. The more I open my eyes, the more I am aware of the possibilities of living all kinds of styles, all kinds of ways. There are literally thousands of ways of living. There are only a few things that everyone has to do; one is to die. One thing about which there is no choice, and I know I have no choice, is that I *will* die. There are some other non-choice situations as far as style of living, place to live, occupation, etc. But there is a tremendous variety of possibilities if you open your eyes, if you are willing to find out what is suitable for you. Not in terms of what somebody tells you is suitable for you.

There are people who are living in forests and caves, there are people living in houses, there are people living in huge 35–40 story buildings. There are people who pour themselves into subways and travel 1½ hours to work. There are all kinds of ways of living. There are people who carry all of their belongings on their back and sometimes throw away half of it—it's too much for them. There's an enormous variety of styles of living. There is room in this world for everybody if you have the guts to discover what you like and to carve out your turf, your pad, your existence, where you can be you.

And of course, if you insist on being "you" in a hostile environment, you're going to get hostility. The moment that I give up trying to change you or your style or your way of being or whatever, I give myself life, I allow myself to live. The moment I insist that ,I change you, I'm in trouble. I know this intellectually and I still attempt at times to reform. I haven't been very eager to reform anyone here. Usually I reserve this for my wife and kids, and you know what, twenty-seven years of reforming her and she hasn't changed. Eventually I'll get the message. Maybe!!

The reforming I have been successful with is with myself-especially when I become aware of what I want, where I am, and what I'm willing to do, what suits me. And when I'm straight with me, I'm in a very good space.

I can be straight with me in a variety of environments; some environments I can't accept and I just don't go there.

People I care about, I can relate to. I find that people you call "beautiful people," are available lots of places. I'll find them if I'm interested; they'll find me if they're interested. So—what I'm suggesting is that you be straight with you, with what you want.

Expectations

I want to say a few words about expectations.

Many times when I have an expectation it is a demand on myself. That is, I'm telling myself I *should* brainwash you or I *should* lecture you. If I don't meet my expectations, I may feel disappointed or hurt. You may like the slogan, "Big expectations, big disappointments, little expectations, little disappointments, no expectations, no disappointments." The point is that if you put a demand on someone or a demand on yourself you are allowing for the possibility of being disappointed or hurt or both. If you make *no* demands or if you have *no* expectations, then there is no possibility of disappointment or hurt. I'm aware that when I put an expectation or a demand on you, I'm allowing us to get into a tug of war. You can say, "Yes" or you can say, "No," I'm giving you that power. Sometimes I'm very willing to give you power and to disappoint or hurt myself. Sometimes I'm not willing to do this. When I'm not willing to give you power, then I have to be very clear with me. Any time that I lay an expectation on you, I am giving you power. If I'm aware of this and want to do it, then, O.K., I'm straight with me and with you.

On Love-Hate

You may not be old enough to remember this song, so you'll have to take my word for it: "You always hurt the one you love, the one you love most of all." In the top-dog under-dog game, when you're busy clobbering yourself, the way you can keep your top-dog alive is to feed him, give him ammunition in terms of "should" or "shouldn't." You should be doing something or you shouldn't be doing something. One of the best ways to beat yourself is to say, "You're not being fair, or loving, or kind"—especially to a person who is so meaningful to you, who is number one on your hit parade.

You can beat yourself by keeping yourself ignorant of one basic rule: if you don't really care about somebody, if you are really indifferent, you don't care whether he lives or dies, whether he gets up or doesn't. If you're indifferent, you *can't* love, you *can't* hate. Indifference is not caring. Loving-hating is caring. You *cannot* have a strong feeling toward someone if you are truly indifferent to him. If you care about someone, you have negative as well as positive feelings. Sometimes the love-hate is so close that you swing from very strong positive feelings to very strong negative feelings easily. To confuse yourself, to play the guilt game is to *imagine* that if you love someone that means having only positive feelings.

On Martyrdom

J: Being a martyr is one way you can combine attitudes or feelings. It's not the *only* way. The problem is that when you pour the gasoline over yourself and light the match, you're expressing your protest about something, and you're hoping that you'll mobilize someone. Sometimes you do and sometimes you don't. In a way, lighting the match and burning yourself up is a means of expressing yourself, of self-expression. Whether or not it will mobilize or influence the other is problematic. There are instances when it has mobilized and instances when it has not.

Consider the assassination of Malcolm X and the assassination of Martin Luther King. They had quite different results in terms of mobilization. There was a man, Rockwell, whose assassination had almost no impact. He did not become a martyr. I don't know if he *wanted* to be one or not.

The essence is that you cannot control or predict the effect of martyrdom or if indeed anyone will take any notice. That is such a dramatic way to attempt to make changes. You have many avenues open to you, many of which have nothing to do with martyrdom. You can try it that way if you like, if it does something for you.

On Pleasing Others

J: Many people think, "I am afraid the other person won't be there when I need him," so the game they play is pretending to be interested in the other person so he will be there when they do want him. They don't really want the other person all the time. As a matter of fact, sometimes they wish the other person would disappear or go take a swim or leave them alone. "I'm afraid, however, that if I get my hooks out he will disappear. So I continue to play the game of pleasing him or doing whatever I imagine will keep him available for the times that I do want him." And the other person plays the same game, or some version of it.

P: I know! I can't stand to be swallowed up. I don't want to be possessed.

J: When you imagine that if you don't do what the other wants, he'll disappear; or when you imagine that if you don't act in a certain way, he will go away, this keeps you tied down, living a lie for much of the time. You *imagine* that if you really say what you feel, the other person will disappear. You *imagine* that no one would be willing to put up with you the way you are, that they are only willing to put up with you if you play the game of pleasing them.

On Being Rooted

Some people are happy when they are rooted, relatively monogamous. Other people are happy when they are going from one person to another, relatively polygamous. These people get their joy from change. There isn't *one* kind of person in this world, and neither is "right" nor "wrong"; there are just two different kinds essentially.

If you take a guy like Fritz who didn't like to be rooted, liked to be moving from place to place, and you marry him to someone who liked to be rooted, you have an incompatible marriage. Marry him to someone who likes changes, likes to go off and do her thing, and come back, then you have the possibility of marriage. If you can get rid of your *should* and experience being how you *are,* there is a greater possibility of finding someone you are truly compatible with.

Section III

Some Issues in Technique

Therapeutic Styles

J: I have a style which I call playing "Follow the Leader." In playing "Follow the Leader," the person I'm working with is the leader and I do the following. I pride myself on being a good midwife. That's the essence of being a good psychotherapist. If the patient says, "I want to be playful," then I go with being playful. I'm pretty consistent in following whatever the person sets up. The first few seconds are almost always what determines for me where we go.

P: Nothing unexpected for you develops?

J: Very often something for me unexpected develops *and* the first few seconds determine what will happen. That is the difference between direction and goal. If you know the direction, unexpected things may develop.

P: When someone gets on the edge of something that he wants to back out of, you follow his direction?

J: Yes. I will never push a person into something that he is not willing to go into. It is almost unheard of for me to

77

have people break down. A lot of people go through
something very meaningful during the hour, something
that is psychotic-like. They say they are ready; I don't. I
have a very deep and abiding respect for where you are
and where you want to be. I don't need you to amuse
me or entertain me.

P: Or to make progress according to your expectations?

J: Yes. I have my own life.

Now there are some people who experience that their
task as psychotherapist is to be the leader and to lead,
direct the patient and then the patient plays "Follow the
Leader." These are different styles.

I think there is room for all kinds of styles. The other
style doesn't suit me at this point. At this point, playing
midwife, follow-the-leader is much more suitable for
me. It may not be for you.

When I do professional training, I attempt whenever
possible to include at least one other leader, so that you
can see two people with different personalities, different styles, using the same framework. What I consider
ideal training is when you see Gestalt therapy practiced
by a wide variety of personalities, some of whom are
very aggressive, some are passive, some are hostile, etc.,
so that you become aware that you can be yourself
within the Gestalt therapy framework and do your own
thing.

Certainly this is different from some styles of teaching where you imitate and become a miniature or a
junior whomever you're imitating—Adler, Freud, or
Perls. Sometimes I see somebody coming on and he's
playing Adlerian games. He can be the most directive
person and not at all as I imagine Adler was. Whatever
the game is, the technique, it doesn't suit his personality. The incongruity, to me, is very humorous; people
get very angry with me when I laugh at their incongruity. They experience me as ridiculing them, and I see
them as ridiculous. We're on the same wave length.

On "I - Thou"

J: I prefer to work with you on a horizontal (I-Thou) rather than on a vertical basis. For me, I see many therapists not sharing themselves nor encouraging the patient to invade the therapist's privacy. In the vertical relationship the "I" remains private and hidden and deliberately or inadvertantly fosters dependency and transference.

I assume that when you come to a therapy (or training) workshop you want your privacy invaded. I therefore ask privacy-invading questions such as, "Where are you now? What's your foreground at this moment? What are you experiencing?" If you are unwilling to have your privacy invaded, please tell me: "I don't want to answer that question now." I respect your right to preserve your privacy when you want to and I need to know this since my basic assumption is that you are here to have your privacy invaded.

Conversely, you have a right to ask me, "Where are you now? What's your foreground at this moment? What are you experiencing?" and I will either tell you or tell you that at this moment I do not want my privacy invaded.

Usually, the majority of the time will be spent in my invading your privacy since you are the one who has come for therapy or training. And there are some sessions, or parts of sessions, where I am the one who is having his privacy invaded and learning more about myself.

The basic assumption in the vertical relationship is if I, the therapist, want to learn more about myself, I then go (privately) to a therapist. The basic assumption in the horizontal relationship is that we are both here to learn about ourselves.

Blank Screen

J: I believe that there is no value in playing blank screen in
    Gestalt therapy where the emphasis is on the "I and
    Thou, here and now." If there is no I, if you play sage
    or guru or analyst, you cop out by not saying where you
    are, and the person will very quickly learn what the
    game is. The game is "I'm not supposed to ask the ther-
    apist where he is, what is going on with him." He [the
    patient] is supposed to say where he is when the thera-
    pist asks where he is, what is going on with him. That's
    setting up a situation where you're always one-up and
    there's no therapy! This is a one-upmanship game, and
    it is not very therapeutic. Except maybe the therapist
    gets an ego-gratification which may be therapeutic for
    him!

On Readiness to Work

J: Sometimes I find the patient is an introjector. He
    swallows whole anything that the therapist offers with-
    out digesting it for himself. The therapist may be insen-
    sitive to the introjective swallowing and imagines
    "Wow! This person is getting an awful lot!" and keeps
    feeding more and more. It is the responsibility of the
    therapist to be sensitive to the patient, and help him be-
    come aware of his introjective process.

P: During the interim today, the question of getting to the
    hot-seat came up. I have had the experience of getting
    to the hot-seat when I feel ready and other times when I
    don't feel ready. From what you said earlier apparently
    there is some value in being there, even though the ses-
    sion doesn't feel good and I am not ready, because
    something is being let in and I can feel it at a later time.

J: My guess would be that a person uses not being ready as

an avoidance and never gets ready. He is what I call the "Promising Patient." [Laughter] He keeps promising and never gets to the point. That is resistance or avoidance or being phobic, etc. If you go when you feel ready and sit in the hot-seat as often as you feel ready, I don't see any real problem in getting enough. You are also getting something when you're not in the hot-seat and other people are working.

I believe it would be a good experiment to work with somebody who would sit in the hot-seat during, say, a period of a week when he feels ready, and do this for several workshops. Then ask him to do the reverse—to be in the hot-seat approximately the same number of times when he's *not* ready, and have some way of measuring, either experimentally or clinically whether there is much that gets worked through.

My early experience leads me to believe that not much does get worked through when the patient isn't ready. When I first came to New York City, I was assigned as a psychotherapist to what was called the Multiple-Sclerosis team at the V.A. Mental Hygiene Clinic. These were all M.S. patients, and the neuropathologist who was team captain would say, "You and you and you and you need psychotherapy. We've got a psychotherapist and you go three times a week." He was very autocratic, and the patients went to physiotherapy, hydrotherapy, psychotherapy, and he had a very good record. No patients died while he was working with them. Very few became worse and had to be hospitalized with this approach.

The fascinating experience for me was that inside of three weeks I had a full case load. I kept very busy until summer (typically, there are fewer patients in the summer). In the fall, again, I had about eight or ten patients coming three times a week. None of these were the original patients! They were all M.S. patients who had heard from the others that there was a psychotherapist available if they wanted one. Here I had a built-in experiment where eight or ten people were assigned arbitrarily without their volition, and eight or ten people who came voluntarily.

Clinically the differences were fantastic. The people who were sent didn't change an iota. Nothing happened psychologically. It's true, they didn't go to the hospital and they didn't die. The other people, though, changed markedly. There was one guy in a wheel chair who had never dated in his life—when he had feet and arms and a penis. He became a swinger, got out of the wheel chair, got a taxi, and was doing all kinds of things he had never dreamed of doing when he was a whole person. There was remarkable willingness to work with what limitations they had. At this point (1950) I was convinced, and am still convinced, that motivation is the necessary ingredient. Without willingness nothing happens. So, when people came to me saying: "My doctor sent me!" or "My wife said she'd divorce me if I . . . ," I have absolutely no therapeutic impact. Nothing happens. People who come who have some kind of expectation of a miracle—they have a friend who changed and they want something, then there is already a possibility that something will happen. So, when you go into the hot-seat, you already want something.

P: Unless I'm driven by my top-dog.

J: There are many games people play. And of course the crucial issue is to be acutely aware of what's going on with yourself and the person you're working with. If a person becomes aware that he is playing a game, he can leave the hot-seat and come back when he is ready.

P: My first reaction was right. When I feel a very strong urge to work I learn the most. I also had a very good experience with you once when there was no urgency to work, and my plan was just to work on my awareness continuum, and I did learn a great deal.

P2: There seem to be two sorts of things that happen after I leave a workshop. There is an immediate carry-over in terms of my breakthrough experience and also a certain amount of relating to the experience which gradually seems to taper off. I've always kept a substantial amount, although some of the high tapers off. In addition, I find that during the course of the year, a lot of change takes place in me, some of which, at least, I feel I can attribute to the workshop. I find there has been a continual digesting, and there may also be some degree of the original high spirits.

P3: I want to share with you that I've had a strange feeling about food this week—I only made the connection while you were talking—and what it is is, I've been very unaware of meal time. Suddenly it's twelve o'clock. Normally I am hungry but I am interested. And while you were bullshitting I was feeling sad, and when you said you were finished, I thought, "No, I just want to go on and be fed . . . ." I feel embarrassed.

J: I have the reverse feeling sometimes when I'm doing the bullshitting—that I'm nourishing, that I'm feeding. Incidentally, those of you who are not familiar with Laura Perls' "Notes on the Psychology of Give and Take," might read it as it deals with this issue.

Frequency of Interviews

I've been interested for some time now in the process of massed learning versus spaced learning, the question of how much can be absorbed in a therapeutic situation and how much becomes an overload and thus indigestible.

I'm aware that this has been a recurring issue in psychotherapy at least for the past seventy years and perhaps longer. As far as I know, there has not been a good systematic project done with massed versus spaced learning. There are some ideas or theories which I think are sound about having time to chew up, to digest. What's missing is some actual experimentation with what *does* happen with constant exposure as opposed to spaced exposure. How did the fifty-minute-hour come to be or the once-a-week therapy, or the everyday-on-the-couch type of therapy? In exploring some of this, I'm both amused and appalled at how some of these customs came about.

Frequently the therapist's way of working with his patients turns out to be the way in which his therapist worked with him. I've talked with a number of people who, if they had had a year and a half of therapy, had the expectation that their patients would get well in a year and a half. If they had been worked with three times a week, their patients came three times per week. These are arbitrary, non-rational and habit-bound ways of working.

Recently some people have been willing to experiment with long-time continuous exposure—the marathons which go on for 24 hours or 36 hours. These are very different from the several times a week patterns or the weekend or five-day workshops. There is a great variety of spaced-massed learning situations.

In our workshop, there are some thirty or more hours which are massed in the five-day period. We have additional activities such as the scheduled encounter groups, non-scheduled informal encounter groups, impromptu massage experiences, etc.

I've often received a letter from people a few weeks later, sometimes as much as six months or a year later telling of how they are still chewing and digesting the material that they worked on. An almost universal experience is that when you're in the hot-seat you can't focus, can't understand, nothing seems to make sense. Then at some distance the digestive and chewing process starts.

Tapes, I think, have a real value in that you can listen some time later and mull over the material again. In addition there is an internal taping that goes on. Certain material remains even though the organism was not originally in a state of readiness to digest it at the time. You may experience it as a very rich diet leading at the moment to a stuffed feeling. But often the working through process occurs weeks or months afterwards. My hope is that you will not swallow anything whole but will instead, consider, chew up, and, where you want to, spit out. I'm quite interested in testing out my hunch that a person can't be overdosed, that with more massive doses of treatment what seems to be missed actually does penetrate and gets worked on in some way.

Self-Discovery for the Patient

[Following individual's circuitous work.]

J: When someone makes a discovery, owns something, do not take away his ownership by directing him, manipulating him or whatever. He can then go back to playing the helpless game, or the paranoid game or the hopeless game, etc.

One of the most important lessons I've ever learned was indirectly from a person who had worked with Fritz for ten years. Fritz went on his world trip in 1961 and the person came to work with me for a while. She said she remembered vividly how she was begging Fritz to *do* something for her and he said, "What! And rob you of the opportunity to discover for yourself?" He liked her. He was saying to her, "You're an important person to me, and I don't want to take this away from you." This is an extremely important lesson. The first time I heard it, it was in a completely different context. Dr. Czernowski was a consultant at a V.A. clinic, where a therapist had been working with a patient who was nutty as a fruitcake, and who had reported doing something bizarre. Patient said, "Hey! Wasn't that crazy!" and his therapist being reassuring said, "Oh, no. That's not crazy at all." And Czernowski turned immediately and said to the therapist, "This is the first time, the first opportunity to allow the patient to get some support," and to the patient, "That *is* crazy; that is the craziest thing I've ever heard of." And the patient came alive. This is what I think happens when someone discovers something for himself.

On Interpretation

J: Frequently when a person is working and I ask him what he is doing, he says, "Oh, I'm just playing with something, playing with my wedding ring." That often has a meaning. Sometimes he means that he is going around in circles, using his marriage to go around in circles.

P: How you develop this hunch depends upon where a person is and what he is doing?

J: Yes.

P: At times I get the feeling that you have interpretations.

J: As much as I can, I try not to lay my trip on the other one. If I do have a very strong hunch, I put it out as a hunch or "I imagine" rather than interpret. My hunches are frequently good and I'm prepared to go with them. One of my primary objections to interpretation is that although I know that frequently I am on the right track when I have a hunch, I also know that there are times that I am not. If I send something out as a hunch or as a fantasy and the other person is comfortable with it, O.K. If I send something out as a hunch and the other person doesn't accept it, O.K. If I say, "I *know* I'm right and you must accept what I say," this becomes a battle, a power struggle between my ego need to be right and the other person's. For me that is a complication I prefer not to have. I perfer not to interpret. This develops resistance and counter resistance—all kinds of complications that I don't think are necessary.

On Completing a Situation

J: There are two ways of finishing a situation and achieving completion. One is through simple awareness. Another is through saturation, continuing until you feel fed up, completed, finished. When a number of situations have natural completions or what is called in organismic terms a "good Gestalt," completion takes place and everything fits. What was foreground becomes the background for the next foreground; the next figure can emerge. Often a completion doesn't take place. All psychotherapies, ranging from the psychoanalytic through the Pavlovian aim at completion, at finishing a situation. The question is, "How do you do that?" Sometimes awareness is enough to complete a situation and you don't have to do anything deliberately, programmatically, willfully. However, if awareness is not enough, then you deliberately go over the situation over and over again, and by saturating, finish. In the last ten or fifteen years I imagine I've tried every possible way of completing a situation and I'm impressed with the way people blind themselves, deafen themselves. I once played a tape back twenty or twenty-five times, the same phrase, hoping the person would finish, but he didn't even hear it. Sometimes completion takes place months or years after the person has worked on a situation. I've had people write me letters two years later and say, "Aha! I finally understand, I finally have completed the unfinished situation!"

On Terminating the Session

P: Is it the usual practice in Gestalt to stay with the impasse when you meet it?

J: Not always. Most of the time my preference is to have somebody work through his own impasse, stew in his own juice, arrive at his own solution. At times, I do something or suggest something. I believe that allowing somebody to stay with his own impasse is technically correct.

P: To stay with it?

J: Yes, to stay and develop his own self support.

P: What are some of the reasons you have for terminating the session?

J: I terminate a session for a variety of reasons: when I feel that I'm at an impasse, when I'm stuck, when I feel like withdrawing, or if the time is up.

P: When the patient wants to terminate, are there any times that you will push or pursue?

J: Yes, there are times when I do: usually when *I* feel unfinished and want to get something finished for myself, to complete some Gestalt. These times are exceptional, granted.

P: Jim, I was wondering about the private hour. What happens if the patient finishes some piece of work in less than 50 minutes. Do you start something else?

J: Something may finish in fifteen or twenty minutes and there may be some indication that something else is going to happen within a few minutes. Then, there is the possibility of completing two Gestalts. Sometimes the signals are that nothing is going to happen, and that is what happens; for fifty minutes! Occasionally the person will feel completed in a 10–15 minute period and leave. On occasion I will feel finished and say, "I don't see any point in continuing." There are a variety of possibilities. Most of the time, time dictates.

P: It's kind of phoney.

J: It is phoney.

Section IV

Working on a Dream

The Dream

J: According to the Gestalt therapy framework, everything in your dream is some aspect of yourself, and in effect when you are dreaming, you are writing your own script. You're saying things about yourself.

Most therapies see the dream as a disguised message. In Gestalt therapy, the message is an existential message, a message of how you exist, the nature of your existence. It usually contains two important elements. One is a statement of who you are. By playing each part you can become more aware of what you identify with or what you disown and if you're willing to reown you can become aware of the parts that you disown. The other element is that there is frequently, not always, a missing part.

Sometimes, the missing part of the dream is a resolution. If somebody is on an airplane and he never gets to his destination, never arrives wherever it is that he is going, *that* becomes the missing part, the goal or the destination. In working on a dream, try to get in touch with your disowned parts, and work on the reowning and whenever possible, the missing part.

89

My preference when I work on my own dream, is to have somebody else there. I have a very sneaky top-dog that is very good at disguising, at keeping myself from becoming aware. So I need someone else's eyes or ears, someone to be my therapist. The person being my therapist can be a person in whom I don't ordinarily have very much confidence. However *anybody* who is willing to listen to me and doesn't want to lay something on me, who has eyes and ears and can feed back to me, can be an excellent therapist for me.

Now one of the ways I can work with my own dream material when I don't have someone available is to put my dream either on paper or on tape and put it away. Then I go back to the dream at some distant time. By distant time I don't necessarily mean the next morning or the next week. Frequently I surprise myself when I am able to work something out that I know from experience I won't get initially. My preference is to have somebody, a colleague or my wife, to work with—to relate my dream to. One of my favorite places is lying in the tub, telling my wife my dream with her feeding back when she sees me avoiding things. Or she might ask me to play the various parts.

P: What about the recurring dream?

J: To me the recurring dream is a vital message. Whenever I have a recurring dream, I am telling myself something that I won't listen to. The dream stops recurring at the moment I understand what *I'm* saying to *me.*

P: Is this true also of an old dream that you keep remembering? Not one that you re-dream, but . . .

J: Yeah. The basic principle is that once a Gestalt forms, once there is some completion, I have no need to re-dream, or to remember, which is in essence the same thing. It becomes stale shit.

P: What is your objection to working on the dream the next day?

J: I have no objection. My experience has been that when I do, I delude myself. I take something which seems to be dramatic or important to me and keep following it, and it becomes a red herring for me; I don't see what is obvious to everybody *but* me.

P: How about the hazy dream? A person comes with a dream that he can't remember, only maybe one or two things in it. Do you have him just complete it?

J: Just work on the fragment.

P: And not complete it?

J: Not complete it. My experience has been that when a person *does* work on a fragment, he is frequently able to complete it without being asked.

P: Where do you choose to begin working with a dream?

J: As a general principle, what I prefer is to take the part that I imagine the person is least identified with. If there are people and places in the dream, I'll choose the objects rather than the places. If there is locale, territory, a field, an ocean, some broad expanse, I'll choose the broad expanse rather than the specific—whatever is the most vague. People do not usually identify easily with vague, broad, general expanses; they identify with other people, sometimes with objects, rarely with places and almost never with intangibles like weather or situations which are nebulous. If you get in touch with the part of yourself that you are least in touch with and start from that end rather than from the other end, there is the most likelihood of an "Aha," of a reowning of a disowned part. If I am working with someone this way and he is floundering and is apparently unable or unwilling, or both, to get in touch with anything that is too broad, then I'll switch to the other possibilities, like people or places.

P: What do you make of someone who insists he never dreams? What is the problem with him? Isn't that a complete blocking off? Because obviously, he does dream; everyone dreams.

P: I had that happen with a patient, and I had him talk to the dream that wasn't there and then he started dreaming!

P2: Not only that. I did that with Fritz or somebody, I have used it with good effect. I say to the patient, "What did you dream last night?" He says, "I didn't dream. I never dream." I say, "Well, the research boys tell us we all dream every night." So, in other words, I'm just being dogmatic about that, and I pull a chair over and I say, "Put your dream that you had last night that you can't remember in that chair and talk to it. Tell him, "You're escaping me!" And the dream says, "I'm not escaping you; I'm trying to break in, you damn fool!" and he develops an awareness that *he* is doing it.

J: My preference is to do something quite different. What I prefer is to have the person say that he doesn't dream, to acknowledge that he doesn't dream. And what I imagine is that he is sabotaging. Any time that he becomes aware of his top-dog game, his sabotage game, then I give him an instruction: "Tonight *don't dream!* Whatever you do, don't dream!" And if I have someone who has a very strong saboteur, a strong under-dog, he may

. . .

P: Then he'll dream.

J (with a smile): People have done that.

A couple of nights ago, I remembered a dream. I dreamt about my mother. She was going to kill me and I couldn't imagine that she was serious. And then I discovered that she *was* serious, that she really was going to kill me. This was a nightmare for me. I was terrified! And then I recognized that I had a message for me. I went back to sleep and I kept that dream. The message to me is very clear. When I am being my mother, the part of me that's my mother, I am killing me. It was very clear and I'm listening, I'm paying attention, as much as I am aware. I have a choice now. Prior to this I would say that I didn't have a choice. I would be killing myself without *awareness*. I still may kill myself but I now know that when I'm being the part of me that's my mother, I'm killing myself. I know some of the characteristics of my identification with her; when I'm being nasty or sarcastic, that is when I'm being my mother and I'm killing me.

P: When I'm being my mother, I'm being the torturer.

J: Right.

A Patient's Dream

P: I want to work on a dream, a very recent dream. I had this yesterday; in fact last night.

In my dream, my youngest daughter, who is about eight years old, gets chopped up with a hatchet. A specific part of her body, her leg, is chopped off. The hatchet is wielded by a boy in the neighborhood that I know, and I'm watching.

She is sitting on the floor by a table and he comes under the table and hacks up her foot, her leg. I intend to stop him and I struggle with him but I can't prevent him from doing this. Finally I wrest the hatchet away from him and it is too late. She is in great pain and dies on the spot.

And then he attacks me, barehanded. I hit him, but not with the sharp edge of the hatchet. I hit him with the back of the hatchet on his leg, just enough to stun his leg so that he can't run after me, but not enough to do him any real damage. Then I stand off, where I'm safe from him, and tell somebody, a woman that I don't recognize who is standing there, that I was powerless to stop him and that I can't understand it.

I woke from this dream in great fright and trembling, the most vivid dream I've had in a long time.

J: O.K. Now start by playing your daughter. Use the first person, present tense.

P: I am daughter sitting under the table and this guy comes . . . crawls under the table and he's coming at me with the hatchet. I don't know what he's going to do. But he starts chopping up my foot, and it hurts a lot. And I can't understand it; it doesn't make any sense. And daddy is there, and he can't do anything about it, and I can't figure it out. Somebody do something!

J: Please go on as her.

P: I particularly can't figure out why anyone would want to hurt me. I am the most healthy, the most natural of any one around. This was an association I had to her. That's all for her.

J: Oh no. You are changing your dream.

P: I didn't do the part where it hurts.

J: Please continue.

P: O.K. [sigh] I'm embarrassed.

J: What's embarrassing?

P: I'm embarrassed to holler out that my leg is hurting.

J: Please continue.

P: Ow, you chopped into my leg; ow, my foot is hurting; ow, it's going up my leg. Somebody do something; something is happening to my leg. They're chopping it all up, it hurts!
      I must be blocking something out.

J: You did not go through the dying.

P: O.K. I'll resume: chopping up my leg, and it's bleeding, and daddy isn't stopping him, and it hurts and I'll die. I'm dying. I don't know how to portray dying, violent death of this type.

J: I don't believe you. [Long pause] What are you doing?

P: I'm touching my lip and thinking.

J: Trying to figure it out perhaps?

P: Yes. How to portray dying and make it convincing to you.

J: See if you can make it convincing for your daddy. [Pause]

P: I can't do that.

J: What can't you do?

P: I can sit and wish that my daddy would do something.

J: O.K. Now would you play the boy who is crawling under the table? The hatchet-wielder?

P: [Pause] There is D sitting on the floor. I'll chop her up right now. Get under this table where nobody can get me. By the time they get to me, I'll have chopped the leg good. I'm really good with this hatchet, too. Kingpin with the hatchet; just watch my smoke. It's a gas, a ball. And I climb under the table and, before any one knows what's happening, I'm chopping up her leg. Every stroke cuts right through the bone; it's great. There's blood all over the floor, it's a gory mess. I've never done anything so exciting in my life! Here comes that idiot father, trying to stop me, and he'll never make it, because I have this table in between. Finally I got her chopped up enough so that she's going to die, and I can't do any more. That bastard! He got the hatchet away from me. I'll go and get him! Ow, he hit me in the leg; I can't run. What does he think he's doing? I can use the hatchet and I can chop good. He hits me in the leg with the back of it. What an idiot! [Pause]

J: What do you experience?

P: A perplexity: this is a side of me I am not acquainted with. If this is part of me, then I certainly . . .

J: If this is part of you?

P: O.K. It's part of me that I don't recognize and don't admit consciously. A hatchet-wielder? That's not my image.

J: A sneaky hatchet-wielder.

P: O.K. . . . under the table.

J: Yes. Does that become a bit more recognizable?

P: Slightly: I've had a history of sneakiness. But that . . .

J: What's just happened?

P: I just became aware of the color of your suit. Yellow and red! For quite some time, I've been working on bringing out into the open the sneaky things I do. And I was under the impression that I'd pretty much changed that. I am very surprised to discover this aspect of being sneaky. Not so surprised, since this is an aspect that I don't recognize as sneaky.

J: Now play the hatchet.

P: Hatchet? I'm about the sharpest, keenest hatchet that ever existed. An edge that will go through bone, can kill in one clean sweep. Just aim me right and one blow does it. Real fine, sharp hatchet—the best!

J: Play the other side.

P: The dull side? [Pause] As the dull side of the hatchet, I am not very effective. I can strike a temporary blow, I can hold things off. I can't make a clean strike. I can't be used effectively. I can only blunt. I can numb for a time, but I can't cut.

J: Now play the table.

P: I'm protection for the boy who climbs under the table, I'm protection for the hatchet. I am no protection for the girl.

J: You are protection for two out of the four people or objects.

P: No protection for myself.

J: I don't believe that. I believe that you are protection for the dreamer.

P: I don't see what the table protects him from. In the dream, I'm in his way: I prevent him from going to his daughter's rescue.

J: Yes.

P: Are you suggesting that this does something for him?

J: Yes. [Pause] What just happened?

P: I put my hands in my pockets. Thinking again. Trying to figure out what it does for me. I don't know what this does for him.

J: What does putting your hands in your pockets do?

P: Gives my hand a definite place to be. A safe place for my hands.

J: Now play the vague woman.

P: I'm a complete bystander. I'm not involved with any of the people in the drama. I am on the fringe of the scene, totally useless. I can barely see what's going on. I can't understand much of what he is saying to me. I can hardly hear his words. The whole thing is a vague, foggy event to me. I'm out of it.

J: And now play you.

P: Goddam, look what's happening. I didn't see that boy go under the table with the hatchet. I have to stop him.

J: What's happened to your hands!?

P: I took them out of my pockets.

J: Please go on.

P: I have to stop him. I'll run, I'll grab him. I'm grabbing him. I'm holding on to him, fighting with him and he is still chopping away. I can't understand that. I'm fighting with him, I'm strong, but I'm not preventing him from continuing to chop. I don't seem to be able to stop him. And it's going to be too late and my daughter is screaming, and there is blood, and I'm powerless. I'm trying, but apparently, I'm not trying the right way. I'm not preventing the damage.

J: Yes.

P: And I blame myself for not doing this.

J: How do you blame yourself?

P: I'm a grown man. I should be able to keep a small boy from chopping her with a hatchet, by taking the hatchet away from him.

J: You can't do this.

P: I can't do it.

J: So you are going to have to figure out some other method.

P: I don't see how. Here is the kid, under the table, chopping with the hatchet, and I'm standing back from it. All I can do is run to the scene and try to take the hatchet away. And this I am doing.

J: With?

P: . . . all my energy, all my speed.

J: And?

P: I'm ineffective.

J: Right.

P: And I'm in a panic, in a sweat, because I can't be effective. That's exactly how I woke up from the dream: in a sweat, trembling, and in panic. Powerless.

J: I am curious about the you in the dream: How do you finally wrest the hatchet away from the boy?

P: I don't know. It seems as if he gives it up when he's through.

J: Yes, there is the key.

P: [Pause] By holding his arm back, or taking the hatchet away?

J: That doesn't work. He's not going to stop until he's through.

P: My attitude is: if my daughter is getting chopped, I've got to do something.

J: What's your choice?

P: Either to try directly to stop him or to let him finish. That does not make any sense. I don't know what my choice is! I don't see any choice.

J: Good. I'm going to be helpful.

P: [Laughing] How?

J: I think the boy is going to chop until he's finished. I think your only choice is to be a hero.

P: That's to let him chop me, instead.

J: Of course.

P: This never occurred to me in the dream!

J: Of course not! In the dream you are panic stricken and terrified. But here you have the opportunity to be a hero. And I'm suggesting this is your choice.

P: [Pause] I'm lost. To save my daughter, that sounds good. How can I do that?

J: I am just trying to be helpful.

P: And I appreciate it.

J: If you remember, in Gestalt therapy we assume that every part of the dream is a part of you. The hatchet is you, both the sharp side and the blunt side. Your daughter is you, you are you, the table is you, the murderous kid is you, etc. All of these are parts of yourself. The good part of you is your daughter, the innocent part, the healthy part. That's the part that gets killed by the savage little monster. And you are not offering you as the victim instead of your daughter. What are you doing?

P: Thinking. This makes a lot of sense. If thereby I could save the daughter part, it would be a most worthwhile sacrifice. I was just thinking: when this comes up in situations, I don't see such a choice. It never occurs to me to make the me-part of the dream the victim.

J: This you in the dream is quite ineffectual: he's a good actor, and he can get panic-stricken, and he can blame himself, and he can play *mea culpa,* and he can talk to vague women who can't even hear him.

P: Who needs it?

J: You do! [Small laughter in the group] You are bright enough not to damage the murdering little kid in you. You just stun him and hold him off for a while. Bright enough to see how adequately you can cut to the bone. You can kill.

P: But apparently not bright enough to recognize this choice when it comes up.

J: Yes. You need the terrified and bumbling you much more.

P: Let's say I am more accustomed to being that. It seems to me I need help to recognize the possibility of sacrificing this ineffective bumbling.

J: All right. I have a sporting proposition to make.

P: Shoot!

J: Go through your dream once more and change it any way you like. First person, present tense . . . What are you doing?

P: Thinking.

J: What did I ask you to do?

P: You asked me to go through the dream and change it any way I like.

J: And what are you doing?

P: Planning how I am going to change it.

J: Too bad! [Laughter] Already you are giving you your usual role.

P: Fantastic!

J: Not so fantastic!

P: This is what happens!

J: Yes, of course! What are you doing now?

P: I am choking back laughter. [Pause] Now I'm really confused.

J: Stay with your confusion.

P: [Deep breath] That was quick.

J: What happened?

P: No desire to laugh any more.

J: All right: What would you like to do at this moment?

P: I'd like to go through the dream. D is sitting on the floor . . .

J: What just happened?

P: I stopped in confusion about what tense to use, and who I am telling the dream to: D is sitting on the floor . . .

J: Now I am confused. She is not sitting on the floor!

P: No: she always was! Near the table.

J: She was not sitting with the table protecting her.

P: Next to the table on the floor, so that it was difficult to get to her and the table is in the way. The person who was most under the table was the boy with the hatchet. So this boy climbs under the table, aiming for her. And what I do now is I go for the table, and I kick the table over. With the table kicked over, the boy stops going for her and turns on the table with his hatchet.

J: Are you willing to sacrifice the table?

P: Oh yes! Gladly!

J: Are you sure?

P: No. I don't know what the hell the table is.

J: Yes, you do! The table is the key to everything.

P: If I could hack up that table, I would give that kid a hand. That would be a real pleasure.

J: And everything will be out in the open.

P: Right: that's where I want it, anyway!

J: O.K. What I'd like you to do now is to make the statement to everybody in the room, one at a time. "I want things out in the open. I don't want things under the table.'' One sentence quickly to each person.

P: I want things out in the open. I don't want things under the table. [Repeats with slight variations in inflection]

J: What do you experience?

P: Pounding of my heart, excitement. A certain amount of embarrassment. I feel unbalanced.

J: Which side?

P: Left side forward, the right side back. As I was going around the room, I had the impression I was talking mostly from my guts, and very little understanding of what this means. Once or twice a recognition.

J: There is a Yiddish expression which is most appropriate now: *Mazeltov!*

P: O.K. Thank you.

Section V

Clinical Work

The following is a condensed transcript of a two-hour work-shop in a TV studio with six volunteers at Bradley University, Peoria, Ill., May 1971. The morning session included a lecture-demonstration and film showing.

Jim S: I'd like to start with saying where I am and what I'm experiencing at this moment. This seems very artificial to me, all of these lights and the cameras and the people around. I feel breathless and burdened by the technical material, the equipment, etc., and I'm much more interested in getting away from the lights and the cameras and getting more in touch with you. [Inquires as to the names of participants of the group and introduces himself.]

           I am assuming that all of you were in the audience this morning, that you saw the film and the demonstration; and my preference would be to work with you as you feel ready to work. I'll reiterate our contract, or agreement. In Gestalt therapy the essence of the contract is to say where you are, what you are experiencing at any given moment; and, if you can, to stay in the

103

continuum of awareness, to report where you are focusing, what you are aware of.

We have a couple of empty chairs and sometimes if it becomes appropriate for you to work with a part of yourself, or another person, I'll ask you to imagine that that part of you or the other person is in the empty chair and to work "as if." I'm willing to work with you on anything—a dream, an interpersonal problem, an intrapsychic conflict, whatever.

I'd like to start first with having you say who you are and if you have any programs or expectations.

Jim 2: Right now I'm a little tense, not particularly because of the technical equipment because I'm kind of used to that. I kind of feel a little strange about being in a situation with you. This morning I was pretty upset because I didn't agree with a lot of the things you were talking about, and I felt pretty hostile to you. Now I more or less accept you as another person.

Jim S: I'm paying attention to your foot now. I'm wondering if you could give your foot a voice.

Jim 2: My foot a voice? You mean how is my foot feeling? What's it going to say?

Jim S: Just keep doing that, and see if you have something to say, as your foot.

Jim 2: I don't understand.

Jim S: As you were telling me about feeling hostile this morning, you began to kick and I'm imagining that you still have some kick coming.

Jim 2: Uh, yeah. I guess maybe I do have some kick left, but I really don't get the feeling that that's appropriate.

Mary:　　My heart was really racing. It still is. I feel very hot . . . no life . . . hot, sweating off anxiety. I found you this morning surprisingly kind and gentle, much more so than I had experienced you in the films that I'd seen. I felt that I could have been either one of those other two women you spoke of.

Jim S:　　Would you be willing to say what you are experiencing at this moment?

Mary:　　Well, my whole body is throbbing. I feel my whole . . . well, it's just pulsing. I'm just pulsing.

Jim S:　　That excites me. I like your pulsing.

Mary:　　That pleases me.

Jim S:　　I hope this is in color. You look very colorful now.

Mary:　　I feel colorful. I feel alive. I felt alive this morning.

Lavonne:　　Right now I'm feeling very tense.

Jim S:　　Who are you talking to, Lavonne?

Lavonne:　　I was just thinking about this morning. I was feeling very hostile. I still think I am somewhat hostile.

Jim S:　　I am aware that you are avoiding looking at me.

Lavonne:　　Yes, because I feel that you are very arrogant.

Jim S:　　That's true.

Lavonne:　　And as if I might get into a struggle with you.

Jim S:　　You might.

Lavonne:　　So the avoidance of eye contact is sort of a putoff of the struggle. I have some things that

I'd like to work on. I don't know whether they can be resolved.

Jim S: Would you be willing to tell me what your objections are to my arrogance?

Lavonne: Well, it's not very comforting. If I have a problem and I talk to you about it and you're arrogant, then that only makes me arrogant.

Jim S: You respond in kind is what you are saying. Your experience is you respond that way.

Lavonne: Yes. Right on. Then at this university I feel that I must be arrogant and I must be defensive at all times. Because I'm black, people react to me in different ways . . . different people . . . and I feel that I have to be on my toes most of the time.

Jim S [looks at her toes]: I was checking.

Lavonne: Well, I am on my toes now.

Sharon: My hands are sweating. I'm very concerned about whether you're going to approve of me or not, and would predict I'll resent if you do approve of me or you don't approve of me, and that's what I'd like to work on.

Jim S: Sounds like I don't have any voice in this matter, really.

Sharon: I'd like to give you a voice.

Jim S: I would like you to do that, and to do that in a very special way, Sharon. Please sit in this chair [indicates empty chair] and imagine yourself as Jim Simkin talking to Sharon. Give me a voice in that chair. Talk to Sharon.

Sharon [as Jim S]: You look scared, and I don't know why you are so scared as all that of me.

Jim S: And continue the dialogue. When you are

through with Jim, go over there [back to her own chair] and as Sharon, respond. Go back and forth.

Sharon [as Jim S]: Now I'm really not feeling all that powerful, all that much like I can create or destroy or something.

[Responding to "Jim" in empty chair] But I feel like you are that powerful, and I am worrying about whether I'm doing this right or whether I'm doing this wrong or what you expect of me and whether I can meet your expectations. I just feel, I guess, about seven years old now.

Jim S: Yeah. Now I would like to interrupt you for a moment. I'd like you to close your eyes. Go back to age seven. Whatever you get in touch with.

Sharon: I'm seven years old, and I'm afraid of a lot of things.

Jim S: Sharon, would you open your eyes, and could you share what you are afraid of? What scares you?

Sharon: I don't know.

Jim S: Say that again.

Sharon: I don't know. I'm afraid of being alone, and I'm afraid of being dependent.

Jim S: I'm paying attention to your tremulousness now.

Sharon: I feel very weak, feel like I have to stand on my own two feet but I can't . . . but I have to, but I can't . . . but I have to.

Jim S: O.K. Check and see whether you can at this moment.

Sharon: Stand on my own two feet? [She stands up]

Jim S: Yeah. What do you experience?

Sharon:	Surprise that my legs aren't trembling more. Now they're trembling more.
Jim S:	Yeah. You notice how you get your legs to tremble more?
Sharon:	By thinking about whether they are trembling or not.
Jim S:	You sound like you suggest certain behaviors to yourself, and then do what you suggest to you.
Sharon:	I suggest to myself that I feel helpless? [agreement from Jim S] Since this is a new situation and I usually feel helpless in new situations?
Jim S:	Whatever your because is . . . [Laughter] What do you experience in your feet now?
Sharon:	My feet feel fine. My knees feel shaky.
Jim S:	O.K. Focus on your knees.
Sharon:	I'll have to stand up . . . Now they are not shaking.
Jim S:	What I'm hoping you'll get in touch with is if you stay with, rather than attempt to avoid or cop-out, you can usually finish something.
Sharon:	How do I stay with?
Jim S:	Focusing your awareness, being shaky, being seven years old, being whatever. Staying with is staying with.
Sharon:	O.K. And needing approval too? Stay with that?
Jim S:	Sure. . . . What just happened?
Sharon:	Tapped my foot. Sort of like beginning to march out into the world and stay with things.
Ed:	I want to work on my dream now.
Jim S:	Please tell your dream—first person, present

tense—as if you are having the dream now.

Ed:
I am on a bicycle going down a street. The houses are very tall around me, on both sides of me. They are gabled; they are pointed. Dogs are running up the street or from behind me, and I am aware of peddling faster to get away from the dogs. I am suddenly aware of being on top of a roof and trying to keep the dogs from jumping up on the roof. And no matter what I do, they continue to jump up on the roof. All of a sudden I am in a kitchen and a woman is explaining that she didn't feed the dogs and, therefore, they are running after people. And the dream ends. I woke up.

Jim S:
In going through your dream, as you consider each part of your dream . . . the bicycle, the dogs, the kitchen, the woman . . . what part seems least like you? or what part is most alien to you? the part you have the most difficulty identifying with.

Ed:
The dogs snapping at me.

Jim S:
O.K. So go through your dream—first person, present tense—as the dogs.

Ed:
I am a dog. I am running down the street. I am running after the bicycle. I am running after the man on the bicycle. I am at the bicycle. I'm snapping at the bicycle. I'm snapping at his leg. I'm not quite catching him, but I'm scaring him. I am scaring him a great deal. He escaped up on the roof, but I can still get him. He vanished, and I'm on the roof.

Jim S:
How did you feel as a dog?

Ed:
I believe your question was what I could least identify with, and the feeling that came up in me is one of viciousness and fright.

Jim S: Are you willing to acknowledge any of your viciousness?

Ed: I'm willing to acknowledge that I am vicious in a subtle kind of way. Umm, umm, I'm willing to . . . umm . . .

Jim S: What's this? [Imitates Ed's hands pushing away]

Ed: Umm . . . Pushing down . . . umm . . . what I want to say. Umm . . . I'm not . . . I'm exteriorly, ah, gentle and warm, and inside I'm sometimes vicious. What I am pushing down is not saying that I am aware of, at times, manipulating people or situations for myself in a subtle way. I see some viciousness in that—attacking myself or others. I am aware that my breathing is a little easier.

Jim S: Would you be willing to snap at a few of us?

Ed: Graw! . . . Graw! . . . Graw! . . . Graw!

Jim S: What do you experience?

Ed: I don't experience a genuineness. I don't experience being part of that.

Jim S: What's missing for me is the snapping.

Ed: I find it very difficult to use my hands, to lift them up above or below this level. I'm . . . uh . . . stopping them, or . . .

Jim S: Ed? See what your jaw is like at this moment. See if you can . . .

Ed: Very tight.

Jim S: Yeah.

Ed: Doesn't move freely at all. Almost immobile.

Jim S: I'm aware of your . . . hanging-on bite . . . you're not willing to snap. I'm imagining that if you did some snapping, you might feel better. That's my fantasy.

Ed: Um . . . I'm stopping myself from doing that.

Jim S: Yeah.

Ed: I feel tremendous rigidity. Oww! . . . Oww! . . . [snapping] I'm breathing heavily now. I either stopped breathing or I lost breathing while I did that.

Jim S: Now do you get any message from your dream? Is there something in your dream that you understand about you?

Ed: No. I was very pleased with the dream. I volunteered for this session on Monday because I was aware of not being in contact with my dreams. I couldn't remember any of my dreams; and then after I had called here to volunteer for this experience, I woke up the next morning and remembered this dream; and it was a good feeling—the vividness of it for me, the imagining, the imagery. Something was there, and something where nothing had been before. And whereas I had felt badly about the void, I felt good about something being there. But I had no clue as to any interpretation.

Jim S: O.K. Put your dream in the empty chair and express your gratitude: I'm glad I had you; you gave me a ticket of admission; or whatever the dream did for you.

Ed: Dream, I'm glad I had you. I felt good experiencing you. I felt good being in contact with you. You weren't particularly colorful, but you were stark, you were strong—your tall buildings, your . . . uh . . . the strength of those buildings. You also frightened me. You chased me and I ran away.

Jim S: Are you getting any message now?

Ed: That I chase my dreams away. I forget them. I

... I don't want anything to do with them.

Jim S: I hear something a little bit different. I hear you saying that you get in touch with your strength ... and then you start to run away.

Ed: Ahh ...

Jim S: I imagine that some of your strength is in your viciousness and that you run away from that too ... as well as in your tall buildings and as well as in the rest of you in the dream.

Ed: I was thinking of myself tall, and I'm thinking that often times I stand crooked ...

Jim S: So ... would you be willing to tower over us ... umm ... tall, and look down on us?

Ed: I'd be willing to try that. Uh, I'd be willing to do that.

Jim S: When?

Ed: Right now. I have a ... uh ... it's difficult ... to stand tall ... I feel that I want to shrink, that I want to sit back in my chair, and ...

Jim S: I believe you. O.K. So you have some choices. And what you choose to do is shrink.

Ed: I do that with my shoulders too.

Jim S: I am willing to withdraw at this point. I feel finished. And I'm wondering where you are?

Ed: I feel not finished ... I feel good right now, and I'd like to rest, and I ... if another opportunity comes ...

Jim S: O.K.

Jim 2:   I criticize myself, my performance, in almost every dimension—like my relationship with people, although I really probably get along with people pretty well. But I'm not satisfied with them, become quite bored. Often when I'm with people, I am very lonely and bored.

Jim S: How about right now?

Jim 2:   Umm . . . I don't feel bored. I only feel a little lonely . . . like, so much I get the feeling . . . like, I'm just to myself and everyone else is in themselves; and I'm just going to remain lonely . . . like going in my little sphere on my trip through life.

Jim S: Are you in touch with doing that at this moment—of staying in your little sphere, and my staying in my little sphere, and no contact?

Jim 2:   I feel there's more contact than usual.

Jim S: Where you aware of what you just did?

Jim 2:   I glanced over at the wall. [Laughs]

Jim S: If you would be willing to stay in the now, you might get some excitement.

Jim 2 [after long pause]: I agree, but I find . . .

Jim S: But . . . erase: I agree, but. Hear how you negate, erase—what you do to you?

Jim 2:   I don't know what it is I'm doing to me.

Jim S: When I say, "I agree, but," I start to erase everything that I've agreed to, whatever follows my "but" is erasure, copping out, dampening. Just then I felt you were very much with me, at that moment.

Jim 2:   While I was agreeing but erasing?

Jim S: No, no. Just a moment ago when you looked at me, you were really looking at me.

Jim 2:   Umm. I was aware that I started to look away, like at your chest or at the microphone, and I wanted to get right back to the here and now.

Jim S: I experienced some real contact with you, and I like the contact. I like talking to you, rather than to your story or to your whatever.

Jim 2:   I like this too, but I don't find this very often.

Jim S: Erase: But.

Jim 2:   Phew . . . I find it now.

Jim S: Jim, you have something and then you start to erase, with your buts. I don't know if you're aware of how. You have done this now three or four times very consistently. You cheat yourself . . . Where are you?

Jim 2:   Right now I'm thinking that I'm pretty much with you. I'm not in my own little sphere and you're not in your little sphere . . .

Jim S: Uh oh . . . Play spokesman for you. I'll play spokesman for me.

Jim 2:   Well, that's how I feel about you.

Jim S: O.K.

Jim 2:   I'd like to erase that. Very seldom do I feel this way. I wish I could have felt this way all the time.

Jim S: I believe that if you would get more in touch with how you erase your excitement . . . You get into something and you say, "Yeah, but; of course now, but; etc." [pause] . . . and now?

Jim 2:   So I'm right here now and I like this, but I also want to get into the out there and tell you what happens to me out there. Do you want to listen?

Jim S: I don't want to reinforce what you do to you, which is rob yourself of the excitement of the now. I'm unwilling to help you do that to yourself. Do that to yourself on your own time. I'd rather experience the excitement of being with you rather than being with your stories. Your stories, I turn off with. You, I find interesting.

Mary: I want to work on my feelings for my older son

and the struggle that I have with him—only, I suspect it is really a struggle I'm having with myself.

Jim S: Can you say this to him? Give him a name and say this to him.

Mary: All right. His name is Paul.

Jim S: Put Paul here [empty chair] and say this to Paul.

Mary: Paul, we have a lot of friction. Every time you go out of the drive on your own, independent, I hate you for it. But . . .

Jim S: Just a moment. Say the same sentence to Mary. Mary, each time you go out the drive, independent, I hate you for it.

Mary: That fits. Mary, each time you go out the drive, independent, I hate you for it, because you are not being a good mother.

Jim S: I don't know about your because.

Mary: No. That's my rationale. That's the same I do to myself doing yoga.

Jim S: You sound identified with Paul.

Mary: I am. I know this. I envy his freedom, even from the time he was a little kid and went to the woods. I envied his ability to go to the woods.

Jim S: Tell Paul.

Mary: Paul, even when you were a little boy and you would go for all day Saturday, and not tell me where you were going but just go, I envied you for it. I envied you very much, and I felt hurt because I couldn't do it too.

Jim S: You couldn't, or you wouldn't?

Mary: I would not do it. I wanted to, but I would not do it.

Jim S: Yeah. For me to have somebody around that

	keeps reminding me of what I can do and don't really pisses me off.

Mary: This is what I do to myself. I keep reminding myself of what I can do and won't do. And then I don't do anything. I'm at a standstill. Firmly planted.

Jim S: I'd like you to get in touch with your spitefulness. Put your spitefulness out here and talk to Mary's saboteur.

Mary: You idiot! You've got the time to do your work. You also have the energy to do your work . . . which you dissipate. You get involved in umpteen dozen things so you will have an excuse not to do your work, or to do anything else that . . . [Pause] You just spend time making yourself miserable and complicating your life.

Jim S: What's going on here? [Points to Mary's hand]

Mary: Yes. Tight-fisted . . . won't do.

Jim S: Are you tight-fisted?

Mary: Yes, I think I am.

Jim S: O.K. Can you get in touch with the other part of you—your generous self?

Mary: I don't really know my generous self very well.

Jim S: Be your tight-fisted self just saying, "Generous self, I have no contact with you, I don't know you, etc."

Mary: Generous self, I don't know very much of you. I think you try every now and then when you give presents to people instead of giving yourself. You withhold an awful lot that you could give.

Jim S: What just happened?

Mary: I rehearsed. I just wasn't talking to my generous self. I was talking to . . . you, primarily. I was withholding part.

Jim S: I have difficulty imagining you as a withholding person. You came on in the beginning as very vibrant and alive . . . to me, very giving.

Mary: I don't know whether I really am giving or not.

Jim S: Say that again please.

Mary: I don't know whether I really am giving or not. Sometimes I feel like I do give and what I give is not accepted as a gift. And sometimes I want to give and I can't. And I feel sometimes I have given too much and I shouldn't have.

Jim S: Yeah. This is what I'm beginning to sense. Some hurt. You look like you've been hurt—in the past. That you've been vulnerable and somehow hurt in the process.

Mary: To some degree I'm hurting.

Jim S: To me you look like you're hurting now, especially around your eyes.

Mary: I know that, and I don't want to do that . . . I don't want to show that.

Jim S: O.K. Would you be willing to block?

Mary [*covering her eyes*]:   When I do that, I can't see you.

Jim S: That's true.

Mary: When I do that, I can't see anyone.

Jim S: Very true. When I block my hurt, no one exists for me. This is my choice.

Mary: I made it my choice too.

Jim S: I am enjoying looking at you. To me you are very generous at this moment.

Mary: You are very generous to me. I feel that you are. I hear you respond to me and I feel that I'm responding to you.

Jim S: This is what I'm experiencing with you. Responding. My style—I call it follow-the-leader. Wherever you want to go, I am willing to go with you, usually. And I enjoy very much going with you.

Mary: I'm glad. That makes me happy.

Jim S: I'm curious if you can come back to Paul for a moment now. Encounter him and explore what happens.

Mary: Paul, I want to be warm to you, and I want to be generous to you, and I think I might hurt you by being so. You're six feet tall now and sometimes I very much want to come up to you and just give you a kiss good night or just put my arms around you and I can't do it anymore.

Jim S: You can't?

Mary: I won't. I won't, because, uh . . . I've been shoved away.

Jim S: You've been hurt.

Mary: Yeah, I've been hurt. Paul, I think it's your own business if you want to shove me away, but that doesn't stop me from being hurt.

Jim S: I like what, I believe, Nietzsche once said to the sun, "It's none of your business that you shine at me."

Mary: I keep hoping that, Paul, when you're 25 or if you go to the Army or whatever . . . that I can kiss you goodby. [pause] I'll try to remember what Nietzsche said to the sun.

Jim S: O.K. I enjoyed working with you.

Mary: Thank you.

Jim S: I'd like to suggest an exercise now, a group exercise. What I'd like you to do is to withdraw, go into fantasy for a few moments and imagine that the workshop is now over, that we've run out of time and you are back in the audience or in your car or whatever and you're chewing over what happened. See if you can get in touch with any regrets, anything you wish you had worked on or talked about or expressed while the workshop was still ongoing. And after a few moments, I am going to ask you if you did get in touch with anything. . . . .

O.K. Anyone get in touch with anything you are willing to share, here and now?

Ed: I did fantasize driving back to Chicago with my friend who is out in the audience, and I had a conversation with him telling him how good I felt about being tall and about standing up . . . and appreciated my strength. I feel very good about what I did here this afternoon. That was my fantasy.

[John's earlier work with this group has not been included here.]

John: I have something. I don't know if it's a regret or not. It is something I am confused by. I may misunderstand what you mean. But if a person like myself cannot make decisions easily and has to agonize over them, I don't believe that I am really enjoying this agonizing I am giving myself. It's something that I know I'm responsible for, I own that, but I don't think I'm enjoying it.

Jim S: If you are not enjoying it, I have a suggestion, John. Any time I am truly unable to make a decision—I really don't know which way—I happen to have a magic coin. And I'd like to give this to you as a gift. Now this magic coin has both a head and a tail. Any time that I don't know which way, I toss the coin and let the coin determine which way. For me, what's very important is *to* decide; what's unimportant is *what* I decide. If I want to torture myself what's very important is not *to* decide but *what* I decide. Then it doesn't matter. If I decide one way, I torture myself with that—that's wrong. And if I decide another way, I torture myself with that—that's wrong. And so on. So if I want to feed my self-torture game, I can always say, "That was the wrong decision." If I want to finish, I can be very arbitrary . . . and find that rarely do I make a decision against myself when I decide. My experience is when I really take sides, I'm usually not against myself. Sometimes I am. It's so infrequent, it doesn't matter.

Any other regrets or awareness of something that's unfinished, left undone for you?

Sharon: Yeah. I regret not getting more involved with you. I regret not telling you that I would like your responsiveness. I would like your approval.

Jim S: I feel responsive and I don't feel approving or disapproving. I like how you look. I can't imagine approving or disapproving.

Sharon: Of anyone, or of me?

Jim S: No. I'm very critical. I can imagine being very approving or disapproving of other people. I don't experience any basis of . . . If you were a psychotherapist in training and you fucked up, I would be very disapproving. I'm quite critical that way. Or, if you do a good job, I feed you some chicken soup. I don't see any context for being either with you. My approval-disapproval is in terms of something that is important to me, something that I judge. I don't experience myself as judgmental with you.

Sharon: I feel like you're responsive to me now.

Jim S: To what extent, Lavonne, do you experience me as shutting you out?

Lavonne: When I was talking to you before and you told me that you couldn't get serious with me, that . . . uh . . .

Jim S: Uh, uh. You're distorting what I said.

Lavonne: I misinterpreted what you said?

Jim S: I said I feel two ways. I feel playful and I feel serious. And I hear you saying that I can't be serious. That's not what I experienced.

Lavonne: Well, I'll say that I don't think that you were serious.

Jim S: Oh, yeah. As long as you own where you are, I am willing to own where I am, what I feel. I feel serious at this moment. And I believe you that you believe that I can't be serious with you. I experience you as shutting me out and I regret that. That is something I am not willing to take responsibility for.

Lavonne: Neither does anyone else here or at this university.

Jim S: Take responsibility for you shutting you out? You are the only one who can do that.

Lavonne: Well, I am shutting people out because people shut me out.

Jim S: O.K. I am not shutting you out. I have no intention of shutting you out, and I would like to know when I do. I'd like to be confronted with my shutting you out. I don't like to be told I'm shutting you out when I'm not. I will not put up with that.

Lavonne: You can put up with whatever you want to put up with, but if I feel that you are shutting me out, I will tell you.

Jim S: Yeah. That's straight.

Lavonne [*Laughs*]: Is there something else? [Laughs]

Jim S: Yeah. I like you.

Lavonne: Thank you.

Jim S: And I regret that when I say something positive to you that you disappear. That's *my* regret. I'm transferring something on you now. I have a 20-year-old daughter, physically you resemble her somewhat. She has a natural. She also has some of your attributes. She's hurt quite a bit. She's a middle daughter. As I see you, I keep calling you in my head, Sharon—not you, Sharon—Sharon, my daughter.

Lavonne: Well, it's very difficult for me to relate to that because I never had a father. But it doesn't hurt me.

Jim S [*long pause*]: You have a great smile.

Lavonne: Thank you.

Jim S: O.K. I want to finish now. My style of finishing is to say goodby to each of you and to give you an opportunity, if you like, to say goodby to each of the others. That's my style. You can do what you like. Uh . . . Goodby, Sharon.

Sharon: Goodby, Jim.

Jim S: Goodby, Lavonne.

Lavonne: Goodby.

Jim S: Goodby, Mary.

Mary: Goodby, Jim.

Jim S: Goodby, Jim.

Jim 2: Goodby, Jim.

Jim S: Oy [Groan] Goodby, John.
John: Goodby, Jim.
Jim S: Ed, have a nice trip to Chicago. Goodby.
Ed: Goodby, Jim.

References

1. Bannister, D., *Issues and Approaches in the Psychological Therapies.* London: John Wiley & Sons Ltd., 1975.
2. Brown, George Isaac, *The Live Classroom: Innovations Through Confluent Education and Gestalt.* New York: Viking Press, 1975.
3. Downing, Jack, and Marmorstein, Robert, *Dreams and Nightmares: A Book of Gestalt Therapy Sessions.* New York: Perennial (Harper and Row), 1973.
4. Gazda, George M., *Basic Approaches to Group Psychotherapy and Group Counseling,* 2nd ed. Springfield, Illinois: Chas. C. Thomas, 1975.
5. Greenwald, Jerry A., *Be the Person You Were Meant to Be: Antidotes to Toxic Living.* New York: Simon and Schuster, 1973.
6. Greenwald, Jerry A., *Creative Intimacy: How to Break the Patterns that Poison Your Relationship.* New York: Simon and Schuster, 1975.
7. Jurjevich, Ratibor-Ray M., *Direct Psychotherapy: 28 American Originals,* vol. I. Coral Gables, Florida: University of Miami Press, 1973.
8. Kogan, Gerald, *The History, Philosophy and Practice of Gestalt Therapy: Theory of Human Nature and Conduct in Frederick Perls' Psychology.* Ph.D. dissertation, University of California, Berkeley, 1973.
9. Kogan, Jerry, *Gestalt Therapy Resources,* 2nd ed. San Francisco: Lodestar, 1972.

10. Latner, Joel, *The Gestalt Therapy Book.* New York: Julian Press, 1973.

11. Perls, Fritz, *The Gestalt Approach: Eyewitness to Therapy.* Ben Lomond, California: Science & Behavior Books, 1973.

12. Polster, Erving and Miriam, *Gestalt Therapy Integrated: Contours of Theory and Practice.* New York: Brunner/Mazel, 1973.

13. Shepard, Martin, *Fritz: An Intimate Portrait of Fritz Perls and Gestalt Therapy.* New York: Saturday Review Press, 1975.

14. Sherrill, Robert, Jr., *Figure/Ground: Gestalt Therapy/Gestalt Psychology Relationships, with Some Neurological Implications.* Ph.D. dissertation, The Union Graduate School, 1974.

15. Stephenson, F. Douglas, *Gestalt Therapy Primer: Introductory Readings in Gestalt Therapy.* Springfield, Illinois: Chas. C. Thomas, 1975.